A "phoenix of women"
Puritan spirituality in the letters of Brilliana Harley

Brilliana Harley was a remarkably brilliant Puritan woman. Of her four hundred surviving letters, Dr. Haykin has selected thirty-eight which display her sincere love for Christ, her experiential knowledge of his sweetness and her deep desire to live all of life for his glory. In each letter, we find Puritan piety in practice through the example of a wife and mother living amid the trials of sickness, civil war, pregnancy, miscarriage, military sieges, the sorrows of missing a son away at university and the grief of writing (with no response) to a physically and emotionally absent husband while caring for a number of young children. The life and letters of this Puritan woman show that true theology is for real life and real life is about true theology.

Joel R. Beeke
Chancellor and professor of homiletics & systematic theology,
Puritan Reformed Theological Seminary, Grand Rapids, Michigan

Brilliana Harley has been praised for her bravery in defending her family's home and properties in her husband's absence during the English Civil Wars and for her undying devotion to her children, particularly expressed in her letters to her oldest son Ned. But there hasn't been until now a single, thorough study on her life and thought. Michael Haykin has remedied this lack. An experienced historian and engaging storyteller, he eschews hagiography to reveal the fascinating complexity of Brilliana's life and times. A seasoned believer, he highlights the vibrant, experiential faith that permeates Brilliana's writings and gently points the reader to the source of her joy, comfort and strength.

Simonetta Car
Author of several books, including *Questions Women Asked: Historical Issues, Timeless Answers* (Reformation Heritage Books, 2021)

Let's face it: most of what is published on the Puritans focuses on men. That's because the men did most of the writing. But not all. With his usual expertise and insight, Michael Haykin recaptures for us the voice of Brilliana Harley. We hear her weaving her deep Puritan faith into everyday conversations. Her letters recapture for us the vital place of women within the Puritan tradition and remind us again what it means to follow God faithfully in our daily and family life.

Tim Cooper
Professor of church history, University of Otago, New Zealand

How refreshing to be introduced to this eminently pious and delightfully strong wife, mother and seventeenth-century woman through Michael Haykin's introduction and publishing of Brilliana Harley's letters! As he is wont to do, Haykin has introduced us to an historical figure that sadly has been forgotten by many, but ought to be remembered, read and retrieved. Through the intimate medium of the personal letter and the insightful context provided by Haykin, the church can be encouraged and challenged by the Puritan faith of Brilliana.

Nicholas J. Abraham
Lead pastor at Reformation Bible Church in Beach City, Ohio; assistant professor of church history and biblical spirituality, Emmaus Theological Seminary in Cleveland, Ohio; author of *Living Together in Unity with Dietrich Bonhoeffer* (Lexham Press, 2023)

This delightful collection of letters from Brilliana Harley, lavishly introduced and edited by Michael Haykin, reflects his well-deserved reputation for in-depth yet readable scholarship. These carefully annotated epistles cover a broad spectrum of topics including family relationships, politics of mid-seventeenth-century England, the proper use of recreation, Lady Harley's health and experience of afflictions. More personally they reveal her deep concern for her son's spiritual life, reminding him to keep watch over his soul, encouragement to be faithful in his public and personal spiritual exercises and reminders to eat well and not to neglect physical exercise. Those interested in history, piety, gender studies and literature will be rewarded by reading this excellent treatment of an often neglected but significant leader of Puritanism. Highly recommended!

Tom Schwanda
Associate professor, emeritus, of Christian formation and ministry, Wheaton College, and author of *Soul Recreation: The Contemplative-Mystical Piety of Puritanism* (Pickwick Publications, 2012)

With a handful of wonderful exceptions, over the last sixty years, the recovery of interest in Puritan literature and culture has not tended to emphasize the contributions made by the movement's very many outstanding women. Michael Haykin's superb new edition of the letters of Brilliana Harley shows what this oversight might have cost.

Crawford Gribben
Professor of history, Queen's University Belfast

Lady Brilliana Harley (1598–1643)
Reproduced by kind permission of Edward Harley

HERITAGE CLASSICS

A "phoenix of women"

Puritan spirituality in the letters of Brilliana Harley

Introduced and edited by
Michael A.G. Azad Haykin

Heritage Seminary Press, Cambridge, Ontario
An imprint of H&E Publishing, West Lorne, Ontario, Canada

hesedandemet.com

© 2024 Michael A.G. Azad Haykin. All rights reserved. This book may not be reproduced, in whole or in part, without written permission from the publishers.

Cover & book design by Janice Van Eck
Cover portrait: Reproduced by kind permission of Edward Harley
Cover background: Shutterstock.com
Photos, illustrations & engravings: Public Domain unless otherwise indicated

A "phoenix of women": Puritan spirituality in the letters of Brilliana Harley
By Michael A.G. Azad Haykin
ISBN 978-1-77484-152-5 (paperback)
ISBN 978-1-77484-153-2 (eBook)

To Timothy Whelan,

A scholar's scholar and a dear friend in Christ

Knowledge puffeth up,
Love edifieth.

Il n'y a rien si divin
que l'amour sans fin.
—*Brilliana Harley*[1]

What a precious jewel God hath in her bestowed on you, and how great a measure of thankfulness you owe to him for his mercy to you therein.
—*Thomas Gataker, speaking to Robert Harley about Brilliana in 1623*

It is (I doubt not) one part of the happy communion of saints here on earth, that the living may (and many times do) reap good from the godly by reading of their goodness when they are dead, though while they lived they never knew them.
—*John Ley to Brilliana Harley in 1640*

---

[1] Brilliana Harley, "Commonplace Book," (1622) University of Nottingham Library MSS, P1 F1/4/1)

Contents

xi   Foreword by Jenny-Lyn de Klerk
xiii   Abbreviations
xv   Timeline

1   Introduction
7   "I found a sweetness in the service of God": An essay on the life and spirituality of Brilliana Harley

Select letters of Lady Brilliana Harley

45   Letters 1–38

Appendices

139   Appendix 1: Thomas Gataker's letter
141   Appendix 2: Robert Horn's letter
143   Appendix 3: John Ley's letter
147   Appendix 4: Charles I's letter

Foreword

Usually when we study church history, we take great pains to delve deep into the lives and minds of great men like the Puritans. And rightfully so. These men contributed greatly to our understanding of God and to caring for God's people. Yet, if we never venture beyond these great things, we will miss not only key information but also the enriching experience of learning from the seemingly lesser folks—women, children, the uneducated, the poor—who are probably more like ourselves in many ways and, in the kingdom of God, are considered just as great. Of course, one of the problems in trying to reach these believers is that not as much was written by or about them, and even less has made it to us today in coherent form. This introduction to Lady Brilliana Harley's letters by Michael Haykin helps us get to one such valuable resource.

As an expert historian, Dr. Haykin will tell us what we need to know about Harley's life and letters. But before we get there, I would love to share with you two specific reasons as to why one should *want* to read Harley at all. First, Puritan theology—mostly studied through the greats like John Owen and John Bunyan—is set apart by its emphasis on personally experiencing God, and though we see some of this in action in, say, Bunyan's autobiography, we get much deeper into the nitty-gritty of it when we look at more examples, more specific examples and more examples of plainer people. Harley provides one excellent example for us to start with as she writes to her son Ned about how exactly to live the Christian life as he sets out on his own at Oxford, by studying Scripture, praying, keeping the Sabbath, practicing self-examination, conferencing with other believers, reading theology books and caring for the poor.

Second, it is all well and good to understand, say, the details of Owen's Christology, but we will never truly understand Owen or any other greats unless we also learn about their unique context in history. Though we may have a keen fellow feeling with believers across time and space when we read about their relationships with God—something we all have in common—there are also many differences between various cultures of various eras. Again, we have an excellent example of this in Harley's letters as she mentions food she sent to her husband when he was away, gives instructions to Ned for tending to various ailments and writes bold words to the king of England and his men in an attempt to protect her home during a Royalist siege.

These two points may seem small and, indeed, the details that make them up are little things, but do not mistake them for being unimportant. It is only when we listen to Puritan mothers like Harley that we will really understand what the Puritans meant about family discipleship and worship—no doubt one of their main legacies that has been passed down to believers today—and in them we have a clear example of what Puritan spirituality felt like and did for the average believer living in seventeenth-century England. And, since drawing such individuals and families closer to God was the whole point of all their preaching and teaching, great men like Owen and Bunyan would eagerly commend our hearts to the care of Harley, a great woman of God.

Jenny-Lyn de Klerk
Author, *5 Puritan Women: Portraits of Faith and Love*

Abbreviations

Calendar of the Manuscripts, I
Calendar of the Manuscripts of the Marquis of Bath Preserved at Longleat, Wiltshire (London: His Majesty's Stationery Office, 1904), volume I.

Letters of the Lady Brilliana Harley
Thomas Taylor Lewis, ed., *Letters of the Lady Brilliana Harley* (London: The Camden Society, 1854).

Manuscripts of His Grace the Duke of Portland, III
The Manuscripts of His Grace the Duke of Portland, Preserved at Welbeck Abbey (London: Eyre and Spottiswoode for Her Majesty's Stationery Office, 1894), volume III.

Timeline

1598	Brilliana born in Brill (Brielle), Netherlands, and baptized as Brilliana Conway
1606	April 17: naturalized as an English subject
1622	Composes a Commonplace Book, demonstrating piety and interest in theology
1623	July 16: marries Sir Robert Harley
1624	Gives birth to her first child, Edward (Ned) Harley
1625	Accession of Charles I
1626	Gives birth to Robert Harley
1628	Gives birth to Thomas Harley
1629	Gives birth to Brilliana Harley
	Charles I dissolves Parliament & begins an eleven-year personal rule of the nation
1630	Gives birth to Dorothy Harley
1631	Gives birth to Margaret Harley
1633	William Laud is consecrated Archbishop of Canterbury
1634	Gives birth to Elizabeth Harley
1639/40	January 24: Brilliana miscarries
1639	First Bishops' War with the Scots
1640	Short Parliament called
	Second Bishops' War with the Scots
	Long Parliament called
1642	English Civil War breaks out

1643	January: Charles I orders Fitzwilliam Coningsby to launch an assault on Brampton Bryan Castle
	Spring: Brilliana refuses to surrender Brampton Bryan Castle
	July 26–September 9: siege of Brampton Bryan Castle
	October 31: Brilliana dies
1644	Second siege and fall of Brampton Bryan
1656	Robert Harley dies in Ludlow

Introduction

Coming across Thomas Taylor Lewis' edition of the letters of Brilliana Harley through the Internet in 2019 was very much an experience of serendipity. Prior to my discovery of his 1854 edition of her letters,[1] the majority of which are to her son Edward Harley, I did not recall ever coming across her name in nearly thirty years of reading Puritan literature. Perusing her prodigious correspondence soon convinced me, though, that I had stumbled across a veritable mine of spiritual gems, some of which were equal to anything one might find in such well-known Puritan authors as Richard Sibbes, Samuel Rutherford, John Owen or Benjmain Keach.

I first lectured on her life and piety in January 2020, in a series that I was giving on Puritanism at Grandview Baptist Church in Kitchener, Ontario. Since then, I have expanded on this lecture—some of which appears here as "An essay on the life and spirituality of Brilliana Harley"—and presented it a number of times in various contexts. In the course of preparing these lectures between 2020 and 2024, I came to discover a number of academic theses and articles on Brilliana, as well as Jacqeline Eales' marvellous monograph on the Harley family during the early stages of the English Civil War, which has been extremely helpful in crafting this

---

[1] With what he called "scrupulous fidelity to the originals," Thomas Taylor Lewis copied the letters of Brilliana as found in a collection then owned by her descendant, Lady Frances Vernon Harcourt. See his "Introduction" to *Letters of the Lady Brilliana Harley*, v. On the manuscripts relating to Brilliana Harley and her family, see Clyve Jones, "The Harley Family and the Harley Papers," *The British Library Journal* 15, no.2 (Autumn 1989): 128–133.

book.² But, apart from an excellent sketch of her life in Dr. Jenny-Lyn de Klerk's *5 Puritan Women: Portraits of Faith and Love*,³ there is really no popular study of the spiritual gems in her correspondence. This small selection from her correspondence seeks to remedy this lacuna.⁴

Her letters have been mined by academics for various riches: insights into Puritan family life in mid-seventeenth-century Herefordshire,⁵ for example, or details about the Civil War in the English counties bordering Wales,⁶ or the

---

2 Jacqueline Eales, *Puritans and Roundheads: The Harleys of Brampton Bryan and the Outbreak of the English Civil War* (Cambridge: Cambridge University Press, 1990).

3 Jenny-Lyn de Klerk, *5 Puritan Women: Portraits of Faith and Love* (Wheaton, IL: Crossway, 2023), Chapter 5.

4 There is a small selection of her letters in *Flesh and Spirit: An Anthology of Seventeenth-Century Women's Writing*, ed. Rachel Adcock, Sara Read and Anna Ziomek (Manchester; New York, NY: Manchester University Press, 2016), 122–143. There is also a interesting novel by Laura Beatty, *Darkling* (London: Chatto & Windus, 2014), which interweaves verbatim some of Brilliana's letters with their original spelling into a modern-day story.

5 See Raymond A. Anselment, "Katherine Paston and Brilliana Harley: Maternal Letters and the Genre of Mother's Advice Author," *Studies in Philology* 101, no.4 (Autumn, 2004): 431–453; Julia Covelli, "'House and Children': Lady Brilliana Harley and the Expansion of Domestic Agency" (BA thesis, Pennsylvania State University, 2010); Johanna Harris, "'Be plyeabell to all good counsell': Lady Brilliana Harley's advice letter to her son" in *Women and Epistolary Agency in Early Modern Culture, 1450–1690*, ed. James Daybell and Andrew Gordon (London; New York, NY: Routledge, 2016), 128–147; Diana G. Barnes, "Wifely 'Affection and Disposition': Brilliana Harley and Thomas Gataker's *A Wife in Deed* (1623)," *English Studies* 98, no.7 (2017): 717–732. For an examination of Brilliana's advice regarding herbal medicine and her medical history, see Henry Connor, "Lady Brilliana Harley (1598–1643): Her medicines and her doctors," *Journal of Medical Biography* 24, no.1 (2016): 127–135.

6 See Susan Levy, "Perceptions and Beliefs: The Harleys of Brampton Bryan and the Origins and Outbreak of the English Civil War" (PhD thesis, London University, 1983); Joanne Wright, "Not Just Dutiful Wives and Besotted Ladies: Epistemic Agency in the War Writing of Brilliana Harley and Margaret Cavendish," *Early Modern Women* 4 (2009): 1–25; Johanna Harris, "'Scruples and Ceremonies': Lady Brilliana Harley's Epistolary Combat," *Parergon: Journal of the Australian and New Zealand Association for*

Introduction

intellectual climate of early Stuart Puritanism.[7] My selection from Brilliana's pen is focused on what she herself would wish us to draw from her writing: namely, what does it mean to live a life according to biblical principle and for the glory of God.[8]

Brilliana wrote these letters in a day when the standards of spelling that we currently enjoy were all but non-existent. She spelled words as she pronounced them or heard them spoken. The Lewis edition provided an accurate transcription of the spelling in her original letters, but I have modernized that spelling for ease of reading in this selection of Brilliana's correspondence. Punctuation has also been modernized, the occasional semicolon replaced silently with a full stop, and a few commas added to clarify meaning. Other texts from the era have also been slightly modernized.

I have retained the Old Style dates from the Julian calendar that was used in Britain up until September 1752. In the reckoning of this calendar, the year began on March 25, the traditional date for the conception of Jesus. Thus, all of the days from January 1 to March 24 were reckoned to belong to the previous year. This changed in 1752, when the Gregorian

---

Medieval and Early Modern Studies 29, no.2 (2012): 93–112; I-Chun Wang, "Personal Geographies and Liminal Identities in Three Early Modern Women's Life Writings About War," *Canadian Review of Comparative Literature/Revue Canadienne de Littérature Comparée* (September 2017): 516–521; Alice Miranda O'Driscoll, "Women, gender, and siege during the Wars of the Three Kingdoms, 1639–52" (DPhil thesis, University of Oxford, 2021), *passim*.

[7] Johanna Harris, "'But I thinke and beleeve': Lady Brilliana Harley's Puritanism in Epistolary Community" in *The Intellectual Culture of Puritan Women, 1558–1680*, ed. Johanna Harris and Elizabeth Scott-Baumann (London: Palgrave Macmillan, 2010), 108–121.

[8] On this subject, see especially Gareth Townley, "What do the religious beliefs of the Harleys of Brampton Bryan, Herefordshire, tell us about the nature of early Stuart puritanism?" (MA thesis, Durham University, 2016); Fiona Ann Counsell, "Domestic Religion in Seventeenth Century English Gentry Households" (PhD thesis, University of Birmingham, 2017).

calendar was adopted—the European world had actually been utilizing it since 1582—and January 1 was declared to be the first day of the year.[9]

The annotation in this selection of letters provides the source for each letter as well as explanations of items or people that might otherwise be obscure to the modern reader. The essay that precedes the letters provides interested readers with further background for their appreciation of the rich affective spirituality embedded in Brilliana's letters.

I am thankful for the help given to me in the writing and editing of this book by Prof. John Coffey, James Dodson, Don McNally, and especially, Melissa Kirkpatrick. I am especially thankful to Edward and Victoria Harley for the use of the portrait on the cover and frontispiece of this book, and for their help with regard to Brilliana's manuscripts. Janice van Eck's expertise in layout, design and proofing have also, as always, been much appreciated.

Coda

The title of the book is drawn from Thomas Froysell's funeral sermon for Robert Harley in which he described Brilliana as "that noble lady and phoenix of women."[10] Going back to the close of the first century, the phoenix had been representative of the resurrection in Christian tradition. According to *1 Clement*, traditionally dated to the AD 90s, every five hundred years this unique bird prepares for death by building a burial nest of frankincense and myrrh. [11] Then, after it dies,

---

[9] For details regarding Britain's switch to the Gregorian calendar, see E.G. Richards, *Mapping Time: The Calendar and its History* (Oxford: Oxford University Press, 1998), 252–256.

[10] Thomas Froysell, *The Beloved Disciple* (London: Thomas Parkhurst, 1658), 107.

[11] *1 Clement* 25. Edward Boughen (1587–c.1660), *The Principles of Religion* (Oxford: Leonard Lichfield, 1646), 32, appealed to this text to support the

Introduction

The phoenix from *The Nuremberg Chronicles* (1493)

a worm emerges that grows into a new phoenix. Building on a long tradition of associating this fabulous bird with the concept of resurrection, sixteenth- and seventeenth-century literature and theology employed the phoenix as a symbol of both literal and figurative resurrection.[12]

Due to the fact, however, that there was only one phoenix alive at any given time, the bird came to be used "as a poetic metaphor for an exemplary individual."[13] In English literature, the culmination of this usage can be found in the textual admiration of Elizabeth I (1533–1603), who was called "the phoenix of the world."[14] By calling Brilliana "that ... phoenix of women," Froysell was surely emphasizing the exemplary nature of Brilliana both as a Christian and as a woman. As Richard Ward, the nineteenth-century editor of some of the Harley papers, rightly remarked: "We are in the presence of a true woman, one who was brave but not fearless, prepared to sacrifice herself to her sense of duty, and ready, when called upon to defend her principles, to rise to the loftiest heights of heroism."[15]

Froysell, though, may also have had in mind the idea of resurrection. So vital were this woman's life and letters that she would continue to speak long after her death. Of that truth, if it was indeed in Froysell's mind, this book is a witness.

---

reality of the bodily resurrection of those believers who have been burned to death.

[12] See Joe Nigg, *The Phoenix: An Unnatural Biography of a Mythical Beast* (Chicago, IL; London: University of Chicago Press, 2016), 169–319.

[13] Nigg, *The Phoenix*, 170. It is not without interest that John Dauncy (fl. 1660s) also called the Queen, Henrietta Maria (1609–1669), "that phoenix of our times." See his *The History of the Thrice Illustrious Princess Henrietta Maria de Bourbon, Queen of England* (London: Philip Chetwind, 1660), 3.

[14] Nigg, *The Phoenix*, 170, 193–194.

[15] Richard Ward, "Introduction" to *Manuscripts of His Grace the Duke of Portland*, III, iv.

"I found a sweetness in the service of God"

An essay on the life and spirituality of Brilliana Harley

The Puritan penchant for curious names for their children is well-known. For example, Hate-evill Greenhill, a baby girl who may have been related to the Puritan commentator William Greenhill (1591–1671), was baptized in April 1661 in Banbury.[1] The mother of Edward Polhill (1622–1693/4), another celebrated Puritan author, was Faint-not Polhill, a favourite name, it appears, for girls.[2] Certainly not as odd as these girls' names, but equally fascinating, is the name of the wife of the prominent English Presbyterian Robert Harley (1579–1656), namely, Brilliana Harley (1598–1643).[3]

Brilliana's early years

Brilliana Harley, née Conway, was born in 1598 at the seaport of Brill (*Brielle* in Dutch), near Rotterdam, the daughter of Edward Conway (*c*.1564–1631) and Dorothy Tracy (1563–1612).[4] Among her ancestors was William Tracy (d.1530), a

---

[1] Charles W. Bardsley, *Curiosities of Puritan Nomenclature* (London: Chatto and Windus, 1880), 163.

[2] Bardsley, *Curiosities of Puritan Nomenclature*, 158–159.

[3] Her birth year is now usually given as 1598, which I have followed. See Letter 14, for Brilliana's own discussion of when she was born.

[4] On the life of her father, see Daniel Starza Smith, *John Donne and the*

maternal great-grandfather and an early Protestant, whose body was exhumed in 1532 and burned at a stake in Gloucestershire for heresy, namely, his ardent affirmation of justification by faith alone in his last will and testament.[5] His son, Richard Tracy (*c*.1501–1569)—Brilliana's maternal grandfather—was equally committed to the Protestant cause. His first publication, the pamphlet *The Profe and Declaration of Thys Proposition: Fayth only Iustifieth* (1543), defended the biblical truth that

> the mercy and favour, of God justifieth: which mercy and favour, we only by faith obtain. ... Scripture sayeth, that this faith, which only justifieth, is only the work of God in us, and cometh, not by any man's power, wisdom, learning, nor that God giveth it because of any virtue, or virtuous disposition, which he seeth in man, nor that any man can prepare himself, or make himself apt and meet, to receive this faith, but God giveth this faith freely, without any respect or regard to any good will, good works, or good disposition.[6]

In other words, Brilliana had what Johanna Harris has described as "an exceptional Protestant heritage."[7]

Sir Edward Conway (later Viscount Conway), was the governor of the port of Brill at the time of Brilliana's birth,

---

Conway Papers: Patronage and Manuscript Circulation in the Early Seventeenth Century (Oxford: Oxford University Press, 2014), *passim*.

5 John Foxe, *The seconde Volume of the Ecclesiasticall Historie, conteining the Acts and Monuments* (London: John Daye, 1583), 1042–1043.

6 Richard Tracy, *The Profe and Declaration of Thys Proposition: Fayth only Iustifieth* ([London: E. Whitchurch, 1543]), fols. Avii recto–Avii verso.

7 Johanna Harris, "'But I thinke and beleeve': Lady Brilliana Harley's Puritanism in Epistolary Community" in *The Intellectual Culture of Puritan Women, 1558–1680*, ed. Johanna Harris and Elizabeth Scott-Baumann (London: Palgrave Macmillan, 2010), 112.

"I found a sweetness in the service of God"

Edward Conway (c.1564–1631)

hence her unique name. Brill was one of three so-called "Cautionary Towns," key seaports in the Dutch Republic that had been garrisoned by English troops from 1585 onward, when the English aided the Dutch in their fight against the domination of the Spanish in what is known as the Eighty Years War or the Dutch Revolt (1566/1568–1648).[8] They were governed as English colonies—hence Brilliana's father serving as the governor of Brielle—and were eventually returned to the Dutch Republic in 1616. During one of her father's sojourns in England, Brilliana was naturalized as an English subject on April 17, 1606, along with three of her siblings.[9] Sir Edward was later appointed in 1623 by James I (1566–1625), the king of England, as his Secretary of State.

There is much we do not know about Brilliana's early years, but her education certainly included French and Latin. Her father's library contained a large number of French books, some of which she presumably read and that gave her a love of French texts.[10] In fact, as she grew older, she much preferred reading French books rather than English ones.[11] And later in life, she tutored her sons in Latin when she felt that the local schoolmaster was unreliable. She was also

---

[8] For a brief overview of this arrangement, see Sara Read, "A woman of masculine bravery: The life of Brilliana Harley (1598–1643)," *The Historian* (Autumn 2021): 34.

[9] *Letters of Denization and Acts of Naturalization for Aliens in England and Ireland, 1603–1700*, ed. William A. Shaw (Lymington: The Huguenot Society of London, 1911), 7.

[10] As Laura Beatty noted in her novel about Brilliana, she spoke "French, almost better than English" (*Darkling* [London: Chatto & Windus, 2014], 52). In the undated Letter CXLVIII to her son Edward, she encouraged him with regard to learning French: "I hope you do not forget to spend some time to learn French" (*Letters of the Lady Brilliana Harley*, 157).

[11] See Letters 7 and 9. See also Jacqueline Eales, "Harley (née Conway), Brilliana" in *Oxford Dictionary of National Biography*, ed. H.C.G. Matthew and Brian Harrison (Oxford: Oxford University Press, 2004), 25:302.

"I found a sweetness in the service of God"

well-read in contemporary theological literature and had what Wallace Notestein, an American historian and professor at Yale University, called "a continental breadth" in her reading interests.[12] She was probably influenced as a youngster by books in her father's library, which had a large number of theological works.[13]

A commonplace book that Brilliana composed in 1622, when she was 24 and only a year away from marriage, provides a window into her thinking as a young adult.[14] Seventeenth-century commonplace books were singular textual repositories of knowledge. Their authors—usually men, making Brilliana's commonplace book something of a rarity—used them to record all that interested them personally, from recipes, poems and sonnets, apt quotes and prayers, to songs, legal statements and medical instructions. Brilliana's book is filled with citations from not only the Bible, but also from John Calvin's (1509–1564) *Institutes of the Christian Religion*, select works of the father of Puritan theology, William Perkins (1558–1602)[15] and Nathaniel Cole's (1584/5–1626), *The Godly Mans Assurance: or, A Christians Certaine Resolution of his own*

---

[12] Wallace Notestein, *English Folk: A Book of Characters* (New York: Harcourt, Brace and Co., 1938), 230.

[13] Smith, *John Donne and the Conway Papers*, 57, 87.

[14] Brilliana Harley, "Commonplace Book" [1622] (University of Nottingham Library MSS, P1 F1/4/1). For a study of this text, see Gareth Townley, "What do the religious beliefs of the Harleys of Brampton Bryan, Herefordshire, tell us about the nature of early Stuart puritanism?" (MA thesis, Durham University, 2016), 39–62. See also Susan Levy, "Perceptions and Beliefs: The Harleys of Brampton Bryan and the Origins and Outbreak of the English Civil War" (PhD thesis, London University, 1983), 140–145, *passim*.

[15] Brilliana "had been immersed in Perkins since her early youth, and the family owned most works by Perkins" (Johanna Harris, " 'Be plyeabell to all good counsell': Lady Brilliana Harley's advice letter to her son" in *Women and Epistolary Agency in Early Modern Culture, 1450–1690*, ed. James Daybell and Andrew Gordon [London; New York, NY: Routledge, 2016], 141).

Salvation (1615).[16] Her book highlights a Reformed concept of predestination and the vital matter of the forgiveness of sins. In Brilliana's words:

> It is God only that can pardon sins. ... None have their sins pardoned but the elect only ... the reason is because none have their sins pardoned but those that are justified and none are justified but the elect. The reason is because none have their sins pardoned but those that have peace with God and none have peace with God but the elect.[17]

Also prominent in her commonplace book is an emphasis on the prescriptive nature of Scripture: "Whatsoever we worship God in, it must be grounded in the word of God."[18]

These emphases—election, joy in Christ's salvation from the judgement that sin and sinning deserve, and biblicism—are key aspects of early Stuart Puritanism, a term that both Robert and Brilliana Harley were not slow to embrace. When Brilliana was putting her favourite texts from Calvin and Perkins into her commonplace book, her future husband was penning a small study of what it meant to be a Puritan. In his words, written in 1621:

---

[16] *Flesh and Spirit: An Anthology of Seventeenth-Century Women's Writing*, ed. Rachel Adcock, Sara Read and Anna Ziomek (Manchester; New York, NY: Manchester University Press, 2016), 123.

[17] Cited Townley, "The religious beliefs of the Harleys of Brampton Bryan," 45-46. See the discussion by Levy, "Perceptions and Beliefs," 137–143. Levy opines, "The pivot of Lady Brilliana's religious beliefs was clearly her belief in the doctrine of predestination" ("Perceptions and Beliefs," 141). See also Diane Purkiss, *The English Civil War: A People's History* (London: HarperCollins, 2006), 144–145.

[18] Cited Townley, "The religious beliefs of the Harleys of Brampton Bryan," 52.

"I found a sweetness in the service of God"

A P[uritan] is he that desires to practise what others profess. Is one that dares do nothing in the wor[ship] of God or course of his life but what God's word warra[n]ts him & dares not leave undone anything that the word co[mman]ds him.

His sins are more than other men's because he sees the[m] & greater because he feels them. ...

The world speaks ill of him & misname[s] him because they know him not, but he little cares for the barking of dogs. ....[19]

The Harleys of Brampton Bryan

When she was in her mid-twenties, Brilliana married Robert Harley (1579–1656) of Brampton Bryan Castle, on July 16, 1623. Helping to broker the marriage was Brilliana's aunt, the ardent Puritan Mary Vere (1581–1671).[20] Preaching at their wedding was the "moderate, non-sectarian Puritan preacher" Thomas Gataker (1574–1654), who was the rector of Rotherhithe in south London, and who published selections of this marriage sermon that same year.[21] Her husband's ancestral home was in the small village of Brampton Bryan

---

[19] A transcript of this document is provided in Jacqueline Eales, 'Sir Robert Harley, K.B., (1579–1656) and the 'Character' of a Puritan," *British Library Journal* 15 (1989): 150–152. See also the comments of Levy, "Perceptions and Beliefs," 134–136.

[20] Jacqueline Eales, "'An Ancient Mother in Our Israel': Mary, Lady Vere" in *Intellectual Culture of Puritan Women*, ed. Harris and Scott-Baumann, 88. Mary Vere's daughter Anne (1617/18–1665) married Thomas Fairfax (1612–1671), the well-known commander of the New Model Army.

[21] See Appendix 1 for Thomas Gataker's dedicatory epistle to the Harleys. The description of Gataker is that of Diana G. Barnes, "Wifely 'Affection and Disposition': Brilliana Harley and Thomas Gataker's *A Wife in Deed* (1623)," *English Studies* 98, no. 7 (2017): 719.

in north-western Herefordshire, close to the Welsh border. The castle, dating back to the 1290s, guarded a vital route into Central Wales from Ludlow, Herefordshire, and was thus of vital military importance. Moreover, the Harleys, as Jacqueline Eales has noted, were "ranked amongst the wealthiest and most politically powerful families in Herefordshire."[22]

Robert Harley had been twice-widowed and, before marrying Brilliana, he had also buried a number of children.[23] His mother, née Margaret Corbett, was a committed Puritan and had taken great pains to pass on her Protestant faith to her family.[24] Shaped by this spiritual heritage, Robert Harley became a prominent and distinguished Presbyterian.[25] And

---

22 Eales, *Puritans and Roundheads*, 2.

23 Harley's first two wives were Anne Barrett (d.1603), who died in childbirth in the first year of their marriage, and Mary Newport (d.1622), none of whose children survived infancy.

24 It is noteworthy that Harley's paternal grandfather has been described as "a Catholic diehard." See John P. Ferris, "HARLEY, Sir Robert (1579–1656), of Brampton Bryan, Herefs.; Stanage Lodge, Herefs. and Aldermanbury, London" in *The History of Parliament: the House of Commons 1604–1629*, ed. Andrew Thrush and John P. Ferris (Cambridge: Cambridge University Press, 2010) (https://www.historyofparliamentonline.org/volume/1604-1629/member/harley-sir-robert-1579-1656; accessed February 15, 2024). This article also provides a detailed study of Robert Harley's political career and the way that his religious convictions intersected with his politics.

On Robert Harley's political career, see also Townley, "What do the religious beliefs of the Harleys of Brampton Bryan, Herefordshire, tell us about the nature of early Stuart puritanism?", 98–122, and Paul J. Pinckney, "Conflict and Complexity: Army and Gentry in Interregnum Herefordshire," *Woolhope Naturalists' Field Club*, Transactions Extra 68 (2020): 1–25. For his biography, see also Jacqueline Eales, "Harley, Sir Robert (bap.1579, d.1656), politician," *Oxford Dictionary of National Biography* (https://www-oxforddnb-com.myaccess.library.utoronto.ca/view/10.1093/ref:odnb/9780198614128.001.0001/odnb-9780198614128-e-12743; accessed July 7, 2024).

25 Harley has been described as "earnest for presbytery" (Thomas Froysell, *The Beloved Disciple* [London: Thomas Parkhurst, 1658], 109). His antipathy to episcopacy, though, is a later development. For Brilliana's critique of episcopacy, see her Letter CIV to Edward Harley, March 19, 1640, in *Letters of the Lady Brilliana Harley*, 119: "I am glad that the bishops begin to fall,

"I found a sweetness in the service of God"

Sir Robert Harley (1579–1656)

yet he was eager to assist and help other zealous Christians who would not have seen eye to eye with him on ecclesiological issues. He acted as a patron for the Welsh Puritan Walter Cradock (c.1606–1659), who founded the first Congregationalist church in Wales, as well as supporting the anti-paedobaptist John Tombes (c.1603–1676) at Leominster[26] and corresponding with committed Episcopalians such as James Ussher (1581–1656) and John Donne (1572–1631).[27]

He was elected as a member of the Long Parliament in 1640. In the year prior to the outbreak of the Civil War, Harley was active in seeking to remove all idolatrous objects from the churches in villages surrounding Brampton.[28] His zeal in this regard may well have led to his appointment in the spring of 1643 as the chairman of the newly established Committee for the Demolition of Monuments of Superstition and Idolatry. This committee had been created to reform parish churches in London by removing crosses, communion rails, candlesticks, as well as all images of the Trinity, the Virgin Mary and saints.[29] Harley was fairly successful at the

---

and I hope it will be with them as it was with Haman; when he began to fall, he fell indeed." The reference to Haman is to the enemy of the Jews in the book of Esther. On the question of whether or not Brilliana was fully committed to Presbyterianism, see Levy, "Perceptions and Beliefs," 147–148; Eales, *Puritans and Roundheads*, 100–111.

[26] See, for instance, John Tombes, Letter to Robert Harley, May 3, 1641, in *Manuscripts of His Grace the Duke of Portland*, III, 76. On Tombes, see Michael T. Renihan, *Antipaedobaptism in the Thought of John Tombes* (Auburn, MA: B&R Press, 2001). For Tombes' mature convictions about baptism, see John Tombes, *A Short Catechism About Baptism* (London: Henry Hills, 1659).

[27] Geoffrey F. Nuttall, *The Welsh Saints 1640–1660: Walter Cradock, Vavasor Powell, Morgan Llwyd* (Cardiff: University of Wales Press, 1957), 3–8. In Nuttall's words, "Harley himself appears to have been a man of ... wide sympathies" (p.7). Levy, "Perceptions and Beliefs," 170, n.119, disputes Nuttall's argument of Harley's friendship with Cradock.

[28] Purkiss, *English Civil War*, 147.

[29] See Julie Spraggon, *Puritan Iconoclasm during the English Civil War* (Woodbridge, Suffolk: Boydell Press, 2003), 73–82. Modern animus against

"I found a sweetness in the service of God"

Puritan iconoclasm

demolition of items deemed idolatrous in the parish churches of London and in various cathedral towns, but far less successful in the rest of England and Wales.

At his funeral, the presiding minister, Thomas Froysell (c.1610–1673), the vicar of Clun in Shropshire, recalled that Brampton Bryan Castle "was an house of prayer: 'twas the center where the saints met to seek God."[30] In fact, Froysell observed that Herefordshire had lain under a "veil of darkness" before Harley's determination to reform the county. "His planting of godly ministers," he noted, "and then backing them with his authority, made religion famous in this little

---

such iconoclasm is often focused on Oliver Cromwell (1599–1658). Yet, as Spraggon notes, Cromwell "was no Harley when it came to religious imagery, and had no objections to its secular use" (82). See also Purkiss, *English Civil War*, 147, 201–203. Cf. also Brilliana Harley, Letter CXXXVIII to Edward Harley, February 17, 1641/42, where she told Edward, "the Lord is about to purge his church of all … inventions of men" (*Letters of the Lady Brilliana Harley*, 148–149).

30 Froysell, *The Beloved Disciple*, 102.

corner of the World." Froysell made a point of mentioning the way that Harley responded to the preaching of the Scriptures: "How would his heart melt under the Word, and dissolve into liquid tears!"[31] To Froysell, Harley was "a great saint by grace" and "if other saints are candles, he was a torch."[32]

Brilliana and Robert had seven surviving children, of whom the eldest was Edward (1624–1700) and whom Brilliana and the family nicknamed Ned.[33] Joining the Harley household in 1632 was Brilliana's nephew Edward Smith, whom she raised alongside her children.[34]

The road to war

The Puritan movement had emerged in the 1560s as a reform movement within the state Church of England. Its initial battles during the reign of Elizabeth I had to do with matters of worship and the governance of the church. The overwhelming majority of Elizabethan and early Stuart Puritans were Presbyterians and were thus opposed to the Episcopal structure of the Church of England. In the 1620s, though, another area of disagreement entered the dispute between the Puritans and those who upheld Episcopal church government and the liturgy of the established Church. It centred

---

31 Froysell, *The Beloved Disciple*, 101.

32 Thomas Taylor Lewis, "Introduction" to *Letters of the Lady Brilliana Harley*, xxxi, xxxii.

33 The other children were Robert (1626–1673), Thomas (1628–1685), Brilliana (1629–1660), Dorothy (b.1630), Margaret (b.1631), and Elizabeth (b.1634) who died at a young age. For their birth dates, see Lewis, "Introduction" to *Letters of the Lady Brilliana Harley*, xx.

Brilliana was especially close to her brother Edward. See her letters to him in *Manuscripts of His Grace the Duke of Portland*, III, *passim*. On Christmas Day 1638, for instance, the nine-year-old Brilliana wrote to Edward, "Labour to keep your heart upright unto God, which is a very hard thing to do in these days. Good brother, remember me in your prayers." (*Manuscripts of His Grace the Duke of Portland*, III, 54).

34 Eales, *Puritans and Roundheads*, 24.

"I found a sweetness in the service of God"

on the fundamental question of how an individual was saved. Up until this decade, the Puritans and their opponents had largely agreed on issues relating to soteriology. In the 1620s, though, when Charles I (1600–1649) came to power, he began to appoint men who were Arminian in theology to high positions in the Church of England. Arminianism, named for its founder Jacob Arminius (1559–1609), had been condemned by representatives of the international Calvinist community at the Synod of Dordt or Dordrecht (1618–1619). The Canons of Dordt, which set out the doctrinal affirmations of this synod, rejected in particular five assertions made by Arminius and his followers. First, his belief that election is dependent upon God's knowledge of whether or not an individual will believe in Christ. Second, Arminius' conviction that the human will is ultimately free to choose or to reject God's offer of salvation in Christ. This meant, in turn, that the possibility of a believer losing his or her faith and eventually perishing was not denied. Connected to this third point was the argument by Arminius that men and women can actually stymie the power of the Holy Spirit as he seeks to draw a person to Christ. Finally, there was the assertion that Christ died for all humanity, every individual man and woman.[35]

Puritan theologians and pastors in the 1620s and 1630s were unsparing in their criticism of Arminianism, for they saw it as a betrayal of the Reformed heritage that was unequivocal in its proclamation of the sovereignty of God in salvation.[36]

---

35 The literature on Arminius is vast. A very helpful introduction to his thought is Richard A. Muller, *God, Creation, and Providence in the Thought of Jacob Arminius: Sources and Directions of Scholastic Protestantism in the Era of Early Orthodoxy* (Grand Rapids, MI: Baker, 1991) and J.V. Fesko, *Arminius and the Reformed Tradition: Grace and the Doctrine of Salvation* (Grand Rapids, MI: Reformation Heritage Books, 2022).

36 J.I. Packer and O.R. Johnston, "Historical and Theological Introduction"

Jacob Arminius (1559–1609)

"I found a sweetness in the service of God"

With the appointment of William Laud (1573–1645), an Arminian in theology and advocate of pre-Reformation liturgical practices, as the Archbishop of Canterbury in 1633, the struggle between the Puritans and their opponents came to a boiling point. Laud was determined to root Puritanism once and for all out of the Church of England. He sought to do so by censoring the press, seeking to undercut a main vehicle for the spread of Puritan convictions, and the enforcement of liturgical uniformity in the parish churches throughout England and Wales.[37]

The immediate upshot of Laud's war against Puritanism was the decision taken by a good number of the Puritans during the 1630s to quit England and attempt a fresh beginning in New England. Close to twenty years later, Oliver Cromwell (1599–1658) recalled this period as a time when the Puritans,

> those poor and afflicted people ... forsook their estates and inheritances here, where they lived plentifully and comfortably, for the enjoyment of their liberty, and were necessitated to go into a vast howling wilderness in New England, where they have for liberty sake stript themselves of all their comfort and the full enjoyment they had, embracing rather loss of friends and want, than to be so ensnared and in bondage"[38]

---

to Martin Luther, *On the Bondage of the Will* (Westwood, NJ: Fleming H. Revell Co., 1957), 59. "The Harleys ... regarded the Arminians as dangerous innovators" (Levy, "Perceptions and Beliefs," 137).

37 For an excellent account of William Laud's enterprise to reconfigure the Church of England, see Peter Lake, *On Laudianism: Piety, Polemic and Politics during the Personal Rule of Charles I* (Cambridge: Cambridge University Press, 2023).

38 Oliver Cromwell, Speech to Parliament, September 12, 1654, in *Speeches of Oliver Cromwell*, ed. Ivan Roots (London: J.M. Dent & Sons Ltd., 1989), 52.

William Laud (1573–1645)

"I found a sweetness in the service of God"

The long-term result was the English Civil War (1642–1651) between the monarch and his Puritan-minded Parliament, which ultimately led to the execution of Laud in 1645 and that of the king, Charles I, four years later.

A goodly number of Puritans strongly disagreed with the execution of Charles in January 1649. Philip Henry (1631–1696), the father of the famous Puritan commentator Matthew Henry (1662–1714), was present at the execution of the king, and later mentioned that at the instant when the king was beheaded "there was such a dismal universal groan among the thousands of people that were within sight of it, as it were with one consent, as he never heard before; and desired he might never hear the like again." Though Henry was firmly committed to the ideals of Puritanism, he abhorred the king's execution as an unjustifiable action.[39] Both Robert Harley and his son Edward shared Henry's opposition to the king's execution. Their opposition, though, had been silenced in December 1648, when Thomas Pride, a colonel in the New Model Army, expelled from Parliament all of those, like the Harleys, who were moderate in their negotiations with Charles I. Pride's Purge, as it came to be called, prepared the way for the trial and execution of the king.[40]

The siege of Brampton Bryan

As noted, the Harleys were full-throated Puritans, but the county of Herefordshire surrounding Brampton Bryan was largely Royalist and thus hostile to the Harley family. As Brilliana told her husband, "I think this county is worse than any, for they are averse to all that is good; yet I do not repent

---

39 J.B. Williams, *The Lives of Philip and Matthew Henry* (Edinburgh: The Banner of Truth Trust, 1974), 18.

40 For further details, see David Underdown, *Pride's Purge: Politics in the Puritan Revolution* (1971; London: George Allen & Unwin, 1985). Both Robert and Edward actually spent a few days under house arrest.

that my lot falls in it because I am yours."[41] In 1641, as the nation began to slide toward civil war, Brilliana stationed guards on the battlements of the castle and brought a stock of bullets into the castle.[42] On June 4, 1642, a couple of months before the outbreak of war in England, Brilliana again told her husband, "I think I am in a very unsafe place. In my opinion it would be much better for me to be in London. There is nobody in the county who loves you or me."[43] The month following, she informed her son Edward that people in the county now hated her husband and as for their family, "sure I am, we are a despised company."[44] And writing in December of that year to her son Ned, she described the hostile climate in north-western Herefordshire: "They [some of her wealthy neighbours] are in mighty violence against me. ... I never was in such sorrows, ... I hope the Lord will deliver me; but they are most cruelly bent against me."[45]

Robert assured his wife, however, that she was safe at Brampton.[46] Despite being surrounded by those committed

---

[41] Brilliana Harley, Letter to Robert Harley, April 2, 1641, in *Manuscripts of His Grace the Duke of Portland*, III, 75.

[42] Brilliana Harley, Letter to Robert Harley, November 20, 1641, in *Manuscripts of His Grace the Duke of Portland*, III, 81. See also her letter to her husband, March 25, 1641, where she told him that Brampton Castle "in respect of worldly help is very weak. There is no one that is watchful. The house is very naked. I do not say this out of fear" (*Manuscripts of His Grace the Duke of Portland*, III, 75). See also Brilliana Harley, Letter to Robert Harley, July 8, 1642, in *Manuscripts of His Grace the Duke of Portland*, III, 89; David Cressy, *England on Edge: Crisis and Revolution 1640–1642* (Oxford: Oxford University Press, 2007), 44 and 48. See also Letter 31.

[43] Brilliana Harley, Letter to Robert Harley, June 4, 1642, in *Manuscripts of His Grace the Duke of Portland*, III, 88.

[44] Brilliana Harley, Letter CLXXII to Edward Harley in *Letters of the Lady Brilliana Harley*, 176.

[45] Brilliana Harley, Letter CLXXXIII to Edward Harley in *Letters of the Lady Brilliana Harley*, 186–187. See also Purkiss, *English Civil War*, 153-155.

[46] See Brilliana Harley, Letter to Robert Harley, July 15, 1642, in *Manuscripts of His Grace the Duke of Portland*, III, 91 [This letter is wrongly dated as 1643.]; idem, Letter to Robert Harley, July 17, 1642, in *Manuscripts of His*

to the Royalist cause in the Civil Wars, the gentry in the rest of the county appear to have been reluctant to attack the Harley family home, which was partly out of their personal respect for Brilliana.[47] Thus, in July 1642, Brilliana told Robert, "I am now well resolved about my staying at Brampton, and I apprehend it is very necessary I should keep possession; for I am persuaded they [i.e., the Royalists] would be glad I should go, so that if there be any stir they might get something."[48] By the close of the month, Brilliana told her husband that she had come up with a plan to defend the castle:

> I have thought of this plan for guarding the house if you please to like it. I would make choice of twenty of the honestest and ablest men that are servants, or their sons, ... to be in readiness if they hear the drum beat, to come to Brampton. And I would appoint some days in which three or four might come to Brampton to learn to shoot off a piece.[49]

The following February, in 1643, Brilliana informed her son that she had received threats from the Royalists in Herefordshire. They were planning to "drive away the cattle"

Grace the Duke of Portland, III, 93; *idem*, Letter CLXV to Edward Harley, June 20, 1642, in *Letters of the Lady Brilliana Harley*, 170.

47 Purkiss, *English Civil War*, 220. On the outbreak of fighting and its course in Herefordshire and the Harleys' role in it, see Eales, *Puritans and Roundheads*, 149–177; Ian Atherton, ed., "An account of Herefordshire in the first civil war," *Midland History* 21 (1996): 135–155. For an excellent study of the British Civil Wars, see Ian Gentles, *The English Revolution and the Wars in the Three Kingdoms, 1638–1652* (Harlow, England: Pearson Education Ltd., 2007).

48 Brilliana Harley, Letter to Robert Harley, July 22, 1642, in *Manuscripts of His Grace the Duke of Portland*, III, 93.

49 Brilliana Harley, Letter to Robert Harley, July 29, 1642, in *Manuscripts of His Grace the Duke of Portland*, III, 94. Buckton and Walford are hamlets near Brampton.

so that she and her household would have nothing to live upon and so "starve me out of my house." There was also pressure being exerted to have her dismiss the men she had brought into the castle for self-defence. If these men left, though, Brilliana feared their enemies would easily seize the castle and "a few rogues" cut their throats.[50] The next month, Brilliana received a letter demanding she surrender Brampton Bryan along with all of the arms and ammunition that she had amassed to the King's soldiers.[51] She refused, saying she had only as many weapons as to rightly defend her property according to English law.[52]

Six months later, on July 26, 1643, the castle was attacked and besieged by Royalist forces under the command of Sir William Vavasour (d.1659), the governor of Hereford, since the castle commanded a major access into central Wales. Vavasour surrounded Brampton Bryan with a mixed force of cavalry and infantrymen of about 700 soldiers.[53] Within the

---

50 Brilliana Harley, Letter CLXXV to Edward Harley, February 14, 1643, in *Letters of the Lady Brilliana Harley*, 188–189.
51 Fitzwilliam Coningsby, Letter to Brilliana Harley, March 4, 1643, in *Manuscripts of His Grace the Duke of Portland*, III, 105.
52 Brilliana Harley, Letter to Fitzwilliam Coningsby, March 4, 1643, in *Manuscripts of His Grace the Duke of Portland*, III, 105.
53 For the number of those engaged in besieging Brampton Bryan, see Brilliana Harley, Letter to Edward Harley, undated, in John Webb and T.W. Webb, *Memorials of the Civil War Between King Charles I and the Parliament of England as it Affected Herefordshire and the Adjacent Counties* (London: Longmans, Green, and Co., 1879), II, 362. For details of the siege, see *Calendar of the Manuscripts*, I, 1–22; *Manuscripts of His Grace the Duke of Portland*, III, 114-116; and "Correspondence during the siege of Brampton Castle in 1643" (https://en.wikisource.org/wiki/Sieges_of_Brampton_and_Hopton_castles/Correspondence_during_the_siege_of_Brampton_Castle_in_1643; accessed July 2, 2024). Antonia Fraser has a helpful summary of the siege in *The Weaker Vessel* (New York, NY: Alfred A. Knopf, 1984), 177–181. See also the films "The Siege of Brampton Bryan" and "The Burning of Brampton Bryan" (https://www.bramptonbryan.org.uk/castle/#siegefilm; accessed February 13, 2024). On Vavasour, see Andrew Warmington, "Vavasour, Sir William, baronet" in *Oxford Dictionary of National Biography*, ed. Colin Matthew and Brian Harrison (Oxford: Oxford University Press, 2004), s.v.

"I found a sweetness in the service of God"

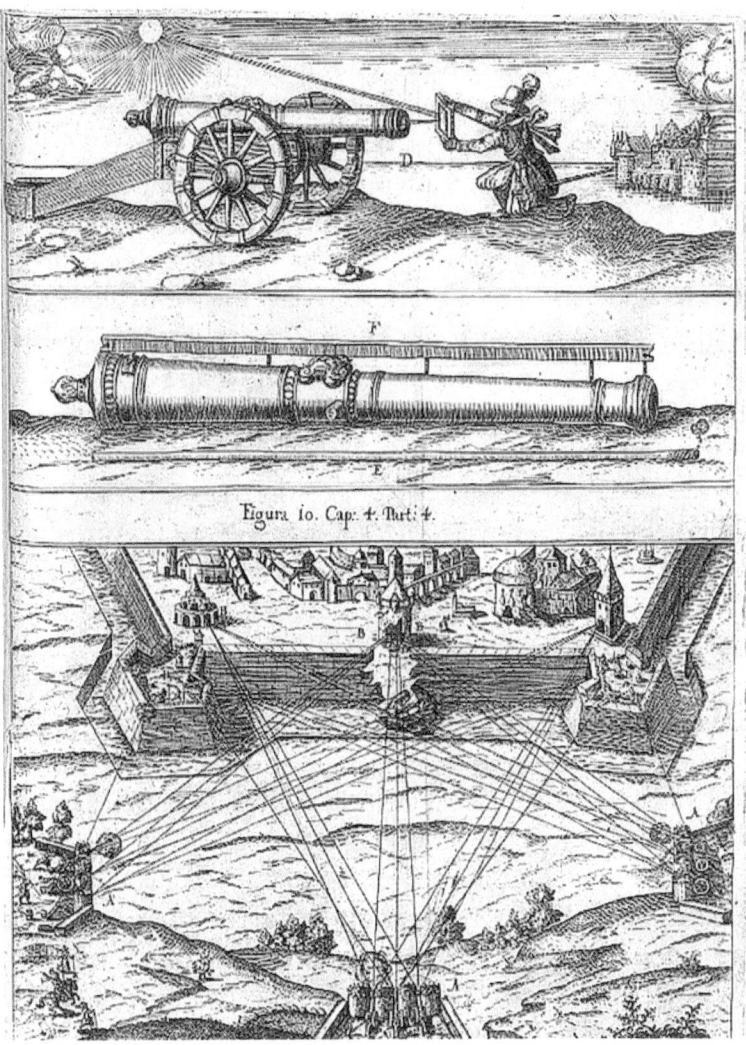

An early seventeenth-century illustration by
Johann Jacob von Wallhausen of the tactics used by siege artillery
to fire upon defensive fortifications

castle were 100 or so men, women and children: fifty soldiers and fifty civilians, the latter including Brilliana and her three youngest children as well as a number of friends. Although the castle was "not equipped for early modern wars,"[54] the formidable Brilliana held the castle in the face of this onslaught and siege till September 9. At one point during the siege, she wrote to her son, "if it pleased the Lord that you were with me, I should then not care much for the troubles that lie upon me, and I think you may do as much good in being at Brampton as being in any place."[55] In their history of the Civil War in Herefordshire, John Webb (1776–1869), an Anglican minister and antiquarian, and his son, the famed astronomer Thomas William Webb (1807–1885), rightly asked, "Who can forbear enquiring, why was not 'deare Ned' sent down to stand by his mother in her distress, even if her husband thought his own presence in the House absolutely essential to the well-being of his country?"[56]

The Royalists burned all of the buildings in the neighbouring village of Brampton Bryan and the castle was bombarded nearly every day. Although the bombardment left the castle roofless and open to all of the elements, casualties were amazingly low—only one death and a few injuries were recorded. The attackers, on the other hand, lost nearly 70 men who were either killed or injured. At one point, Brilliana discovered the Royalists were planning to fire on the castle with grenades. In an audacious move, on August 21, she sent ten men out of the castle to find the building in which the

---

[54] I-Chun Wang, "Personal Geographies and Liminal Identities in Three Early Modern Women's Life Writings About War," *Canadian Review of Comparative Literaure/Revue Canadienne de Littérature Comparée* (September 2017): 517–518.

[55] Brilliana Harley, Letter to Edward Harley, undated, in Webb and Webb, *Memorials of the Civil War*, II, 362.

[56] Webb and Webb, *Memorials of the Civil War*, II, 362.

grenades were being kept. They did so and were able to destroy all of the grenades.[57]

The king himself, Charles I, wrote Brilliana on the same day, encouraging her to surrender.[58] But she refused. As she had stated at the beginning of the siege, the king, at his coronation, had made

> many solemn promises that he would maintain the laws and liberties of this kingdom. I cannot then think he would give a command to take anything away from his loyal subject, and much less to take away my house. ... I must endeavor to keep what is mine as well as I can, in which I have the law of nature, of reason, and of the land on my side, and you [that is, the King and his troops] none to take it from me.[59]

The siege was lifted on September 9, when the Royalists left to join an ongoing siege of the city of Gloucester. A second siege took place in the spring of 1644. This time the Royalists prevailed and took the castle after only three weeks. Using mines and more powerful artillery, the Royalists inflicted substantial damage upon the castle. The siege ended when the castle was surrendered to the attacking forces. The building was sacked and burned—the ruins are there to this day—and sixty-seven prisoners were taken to Shrewsbury for a year.[60]

---

57 Priamus Davies, "An account of the sieges of Brampton Castle and the massacre of Hopton Castle" in *Calendar of the Manuscripts*, I, 25; Notestein, *English Folk*, 257.

58 For his letter, see Appendix 4.

59 See Letter 36.

60 For details of this second siege and the destruction of the castle, see John Webb and T.W. Webb, *Memorials of the Civil War Between King Charles I and the Parliament of England as it Affected Herefordshire and the Adjacent Counties* (London: Longmans, Green, and Co., 1879), II, 359–363 and 13–15.

Brilliana, though, was not alive to witness the surrender of the castle, for she had died the previous autumn, on October 29, 1643. In what appears to be her final letter to her husband, she told him:

> It has pleased God to exercise me with many troubles but my God has not yet left me, and I hope he will not. Dear Sir pray for me, for I have great need of it, that the Lord would never leave me to myself, but to guide me by his wisdom that I may be able to deal with the subtle and malicious enemies that are against me. ... All the children are well but I have taken an exceeding great cold which much troubles me.[61]

Along with the "exceeding great cold" that afflicted Brilliana, she had an attack of kidney stones about a week before her death. On Saturday, October 28, she suffered a stroke and experienced convulsions. She seemed to be recovering from these, but toward the evening on Sunday, October 29, "the sweet lady's soul," Samuel More (1594–1662), a Parliamentary soldier, wrote, "went to keep the eternal Sabbath in heaven, where she can never be besieged."[62] The cause of death was later described by Priamus Davies (*fl.*1642–1661), a relative of the Harleys and professional soldier who had aided Brilliana in her defence of Brampton Bryan, as "an apoplexy, with a defluxion of the lungs."[63]

---

[61] Brilliana Harley, Letter to Robert Harley, October 16, 1643, in *Manuscripts of His Grace the Duke of Portland*, III, 117. In her last letter to her son, Brilliana told Ned: "My trust is only in my God, who never yet failed me." (Letter CCV, October 9, 1643, in *Letters of the Lady Brilliana Harley*, 209.

[62] Samuel More, Letter to Richard Sankey, October 29, 1643, in *Manuscripts of His Grace the Duke of Portland*, III, 118.

[63] Davies, "Account of the sieges of Brampton Castle" in *Calendar of the Manuscripts*, I, 27. Davies had nothing but admiration for Brilliana:

"I found a sweetness in the service of God"

This drawing of the ruins of Brampton Bryan Castle was done by Samuel and Nathaniel Buck in *A Collection of Engravings of Castles, and Abbeys in England* ([London:] Golden Buck, 1732), which was funded by subscription. This drawing appeared as no.22 in their "Seventh set of Twenty-Four Views."

Brilliana had given instructions for her body to be "wrapped in lead" and placed in "a high tower of the castle" until such a time that was appropriate for her funeral.[64] Due to the siege

> This noble lady who commanded in chief, I may truly say with such a masculine bravery, both for religion, resolution, wisdom and warlike policy, that her equal I never yet saw ... her gallant resolution, her admirable wisdom in government, her earnest zeal in religion, her care of all our preservations, her encouragement in greatest difficulties had so drawn all our hearts to the admiration and honour of her perfections, that her commands carried us into the cannon's mouth; in short her word was a law to us (Davies, "Account of the sieges of Brampton Castle" in *Calendar of the Manuscripts*, I, 27–28).

And as he told Edward Harley on July 3, 1643: "had I a thousand lives I would—so far as I know mine own heart—lay them all down in her service and defence" (*Manuscripts of His Grace the Duke of Portland*, III, 111).

[64] Davies, "Account of the sieges of Brampton Castle" in *Calendar of the Manuscripts*, I, 27–28.

Puritan spirituality in the letters of Brilliana Harley

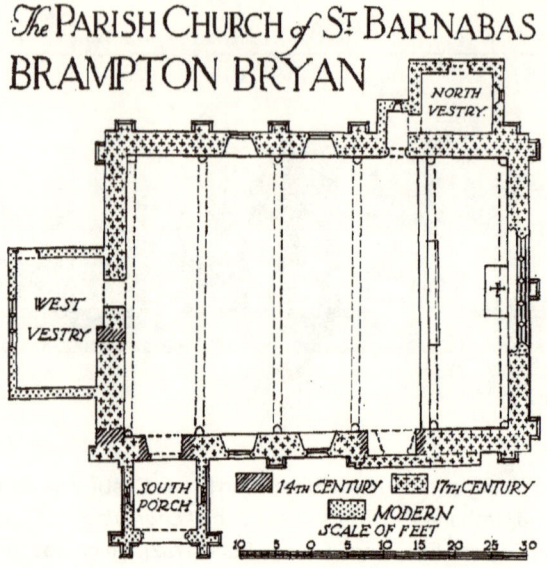

The floorplan of St. Barnabas Church, Brampton Bryan

St. Barnabas Church today

the following year, that time never came. The place of her burial is thus unknown. There has been speculation that her body was interred in a vault within St. Barnabas Church in Brampton Bryan after the church, which had been largely destroyed during the siege, was rebuilt during the Commonwealth Period (1649–1660). No gravesite has yet been found.

Edward Harley

Brilliana was "a skilled and prodigious letter writer."[65] Some 400 of her letters written from 1623 until her death in October 1643 have survived. They provide a detailed picture of her married life, the outbreak of the Civil War in Herefordshire, and the life of a family at odds with local political sentiment. In the words of Justine Jordan, fiction editor at *The Guardian*: "Her longing for her absent husband, fierce love for her children and fury when her neighbours turn on her ... blaze off the page."[66] The majority of her extant letters are to her eldest son, Edward, or Ned, as she calls him, to whom she wrote weekly while he was at Oxford from 1638 to 1640.

Edward Harley, Brilliana and Robert's eldest son, went up to Magdalen Hall at Oxford University in 1638, which was to Oxford what Emmanuel College was to Cambridge, namely, a seedbed for Puritanism.[67] He stayed at Oxford for two years,

---

[65] Justine Jordan, "*Darkling* by Laura Beatty review—a 17th-century Puritan provides solace," *The Guardian* (June 7, 2014) (https://www.theguardian.com/books/2014/jun/07/darkling-women-brilliana-harley-laura-beatty-novel-review; accessed June 25, 2024).

[66] Jordan, "*Darkling* by Laura Beatty review."

[67] Lewis, "Introduction" to *Letters of the Lady Brilliana Harley*, xx; Angus McInnes, *Robert Harley, Puritan Politician* (London: Victor Gollancz Ltd., 1970), 21. For Edward Harley's life, see Lewis, "Introduction" to *Letters of the Lady Brilliana Harley*, xx–xxix. His son, Robert Harley (1661–1724), is sometimes described as England's first prime minister and is connected to the development of the famous Harley Street in London.

Sir Edward Harley (1624–1700)

"I found a sweetness in the service of God"

but left in 1640 without receiving a degree.[68] When the Civil War broke out in 1642, he fought with the Parliamentary armies. With his father, he supported the Presbyterians and due to their opposition to the trial of the king, he and his father fell out of favour with Cromwell and the government of the Commonwealth. He supported the Restoration of Charles II, but also advocated for the religious toleration of non-Anglicans, known as Dissenters or Nonconformists.[69]

From 1660 onward, Edward was a member of Parliament during the reigns of Charles II and William III. And while he attended the state church, he also went to hear the preaching of Puritan ministers like Richard Baxter (1615–1691). He counted among his friends, the poet Thomas Traherne (1636/1637–1674).[70] According to one account of his life, Edward Harley developed "a very Christian temper" and was "a good and religious man, untainted by the evils of that most licentious age."[71] This was owing, this account continued, to God's grace and his constant reading of the Scriptures.[72] But one also must think of the way that God used the influence of his mother's piety.

Brilliana's spirituality

The spirituality of Brilliana Harley was grounded in the Calvinist soil of England's Puritan world: centred upon the

---

68 Purkiss, *English Civil War*, 150.
69 Lewis, "Introduction" to *Letters of the Lady Brilliana Harley*, xxv.
70 "Sir Edward Harley's Retrospect on the Completion of his Fiftieth Year" in *Letters of the Lady Brilliana Harley*, 249.
71 Lewis, "Introduction" to *Letters of the Lady Brilliana Harley*, xxvi. For two snapshots of his piety, see "Sir Edward Harley's Retrospect of his Life on entering his Fiftieth Year. 21 Oct. 1673" and "Sir Edward Harley's Retrospect on the Completion of his Fiftieth Year" in *Letters of the Lady Brilliana Harley*, 247–250. See also McInnes, *Robert Harley, Puritan Politician*, 21–25.
72 Lewis, "Introduction" to *Letters of the Lady Brilliana Harley*, xxvi.

sovereignty of God in salvation and all of life with its ultimate *telos* being God's glory. As she wrote in her Commonplace Book in 1622: "It is God that first turns our will to that which is good and we are converted by the power of God only."[73] Seventeen years later, a prayer for her son revealed the same conviction about the sovereignty of God and also, the end for which all creatures exist:

> I beseech the Lord who has your times in his hand and is the preserver of man, that he would add many years to your life, that you may be full of days and full of grace, that you may live here to the glory of your God, to which end you were made and that after this life you may inherit eternity.[74]

In her convictions regarding these two key elements of the Christian faith, she was actually reproducing what had been central to the theology of John Calvin, with whose writings, as has been noted, she was quite familiar.[75]

Brilliana's conviction of the necessity of the insuperable work of God in conversion was tied to her Augustinian conception of the innate sinfulness of humanity. In her letters to her son, she warned him about the dangers of sin. "Nothing hurts the soul like that deadly poison of sin," she told him in the summer of 1639.[76] And that fall, she urged him: "let it be your resolution and practice in your life, rather to die than sin against your gracious and holy God. We have so gracious

---

[73] Cited Purkiss, *English Civil War*, 144–145.
[74] Brilliana Harley, Letter L to Edward Harley, October 24, 1639, in *Letters of the Lady Brilliana Harley*, 66. See also Brilliana Harley, Letter CLIV to Edward Harley, May 17, 1642, in *Letters of the Lady Brilliana Harley*, 161: "I pray God compose things to his glory and his church's advantage."
[75] See also Letter 11.
[76] See Letter 26.

"I found a sweetness in the service of God"

a God, that nothing can put a distance between him and our souls, but sin; watch therefore against that enemy."[77] In fact, she asserted, "it was sin that crucified our Lord."[78]

So dire was this human situation that only divine help could free the will and re-fashion the affections. It is no surprise, therefore, that Brilliana was strongly committed to the doctrine of unconditional election, which was also central to the debate with both Dutch and English Arminianism. Thus, Brilliana prayed in November 1638 that her son would be a recipient of those "choice blessings of his Spirit, which none but his dear elect are partakers of; that so you may taste that sweetness in God's service which indeed is in it: but the men of this world cannot perceive it."[79] It is significant that Brilliana yokes together here the doctrine of election with the believer's experience. Her conviction about election did not simply entail an intellectual commitment to the doctrine but was one that was profoundly experiential. Again, she reminded Ned that the experience of the "love of the Lord is not common to all."[80] To be sure, divine mercies are the common experience for all human beings, but only some, the elect, know their origin. As she put it:

> None are partakers of his love but his children; and he so loved them, that he gave his Son to die for them. O that we could but see the depth of that love of God in Christ to us: then sure, love would constrain us to serve the Lord, with all our hearts most willingly.[81]

---

77 Brilliana Harley, Letter LIV to Edward Harley. November 4, 1639, in *Letters of the Lady Brilliana Harley*, 71. See also the discussion of Brilliana's warnings about sin by Johanna Harris, "Be plyeabell to all good counsel," 134–139.
78 See Letter 11.
79 See Letter 5. See also Letter 18.
80 See Letter 11.
81 See Letter 11.

Once again, Brilliana moved seamlessly from the concept of divine election to human affections. In this case, she reflected on the fact that personal assurance of Christ's atoning death should issue in whole-hearted service to Christ and to God.

Brilliana's loves

At every turn, Brilliana's letters bear witness to a passionate soul and an affective piety. There is her deep love for her husband. In a letter written in 1628, for instance, she stated: "I much long to hear from you, but more a thousand times to see you, which I presume you will not believe, because you cannot possibly measure my love. ... If I thought it would hasten your coming home, I would entreat you to do so."[82] As Jacqueline Eales has noted, Brilliana "clearly valued her husband's company and the times when he was absent from her were keenly felt."[83] When her second son, Robert, was born in 1626, her husband was not at home for the christening and his naming. Brilliana informed him that she had called him by the name that "I love best, being yours."[84] Sixteen years later, her love for Robert was just as ardent and unabated: "You are the great comfort of my life," she told him in May 1642.[85] Since we do not have any of Robert's letters to Brilliana—she may well have destroyed them during the siege lest they fall into enemy hands—historians have been divided over whether or not the depth of Brilliana's love was reciprocated. Jacqueline Eales and Anthony Fletcher are of the opinion that Robert's love for his wife deepened with the

---

[82] Brilliana Harley, Letter V to Robert Harley in *Letters of the Lady Brilliana Harley*, 4.

[83] Eales, *Puritans and Roundheads*, 23.

[84] Brilliana Harley, Letter to Robert Harley, April 21, 1626, in *Manuscripts of His Grace the Duke of Portland*, III, 21.

[85] Brilliana Harley, Letter to Robert Harley, May 17, 1642, cited Laura Beatty, *Darkling* (London: Chatto & Windus, 2014), 266.

passing years.[86] On the other hand, nineteenth-century students of Brilliana's letters were not so sanguine. Richard Ward commented about Robert's absence from the siege of Brampton Bryan: "It is difficult for us to understand why he did not either permit her to go away or take some active steps for the protection of his family." [87] And the Webbs, father and son, reasoned on the basis of the extant correspondence of Brilliana to her husband:

> It is difficult to peruse the most interesting series of letters published by the Camden Society without an impression that the course of years and events had somewhat impaired the warmth of conjugal affection which had evidently existed at an earlier and less distracted period. Correspondence between herself and her husband was not indeed altogether intermitted, but "deare Ned" had become the principal depositary of her anxieties and distresses, many important requests were transmitted to the husband through the son, and to him were addressed those sad and touching regrets, chastened by the most devout submission to the Divine Will, which give to these letters their peculiar charm. The fact of her unaided and uncheered desolation at Brampton points in the same direction.[88]

Brilliana's letters also bear witness to her deep love for her son, affectionately called Ned. They are replete with concern

---

[86] Eales, *Puritans and Roundheads*, 21–23; Anthony Fletcher, *Gender, Sex and Subordination in England 1500–1800* (New Haven, CT; London: Yale University Press, 1995), 158–159.

[87] Ward, "Introduction" to *Manuscripts of His Grace the Duke of Portland*, III, iv.

[88] Webb and Webb, *Memorials of the Civil War*, II, 362.

of the parlement nor saints when he writs
he says nothing of your father nor of the
parlement.
I pray God give the two howses a happy
union together for the Effects of this parlem[ent]
will not be indifferent neither good nor [evil]
but Either very good or Ells the Contrary.
The deputy lieftenants have bine at Harford
aboute sending the souldiers Captaine Button is to
Captaine of them he is as they say a proper
Gentellman. Roger Gock was wilde for his
Brother bring Gris Snu I could not prevaile
The wise Counstabell of Brownm and was Constra[ined]
to send Semuell to the deputy lesteneants they thou[ght]
it much that I could not Command that of
him, which if I had sent to any Gentell man
in the Cuntry they would have done more as
they said: the soulders are very unruly.
I thinke God your Brothers and Sisters are well
and Edward Piner is a Brood a gaine.
Good Docter Backer is as thay say sick to Death
Bleghly has thees 2 dayes bin in ginious disp[ute]
and is in ginious agony of Conscience and dispa[ire]
Shee says shee shall be demned desire Mr pith[?]
to pray for her and Deare Ned pray fa[ther]
that was with me and for her desire was bi[ng]
to see me and to speake with me

my Deare Ned, Sorry to See me as I doo to
you but the Lord in mercy giue me
Comfortabell Seeing you which is much
desierd by

your

Most Affectionat Mother

Brilliana Harley

Deare Ned remember me
to your worthy Tutor
If you doo not Come home at
Witsentide I would haue you send
me one of your shirts and to
take more then 3 and I will
if pleas God send them you
I like the Coate very well

May: y:
1640
Bromton Castell

One of Brilliana's letters showing her signature

Puritan spirituality in the letters of Brilliana Harley

for his physical health,[89] advice regarding his diet and medicine[90] and notification of gifts of food being sent from Brampton to Oxford.[91] Seamlessly intermingled with such mundane matters are precepts for godly living,[92] nuggets of spiritual advice and discussion of books the two of them have been reading. The latter are especially intriguing and reveal Brilliana to have been a voracious reader with a wide variety of literary interests ranging from theological treatises by celebrated authors like Calvin and Perkins to Roman Catholic works, from pamphlets containing the latest news to works of fiction like the fantasy by Francis Godwin (1562–1633), *The man in the Moone*. In her spiritual advice to her son, a number of items are especially prominent: the importance of regular communion with God in prayer[93] and the private reading of Scripture, "the sweet waters of God's Word,"[94] and other devotional works. Brilliana encouraged him to be earnest in observing the Sabbath,[95] though Edward complained that he could not find a preaching ministry as powerful as that which he had enjoyed at Brampton.[96] What is conspicuous by its absence, though, is any reference to the Lord's Supper.[97]

Finally, there is Brilliana's love for her God. Rooted firmly in God's Word and the Augustinian tradition of Puritanism, it was unashamedly affective and experiential. Her use of the

---

[89] See, for example, Letters 7, 8, 9, 10, 14, 21 and 26.
[90] See, for example, Letters 5, 9 and 24.
[91] See, for example, Letters 6, 7 and 27.
[92] Fletcher, *Gender, Sex and Subordination*, 137.
[93] See, for example, Letters 8, 11, 16 and 27.
[94] See, for example, Letters 2, 8, 11 and 17.
[95] See, for example, Letters 4 and 16. Cf. also Letter 28.
[96] See Letter 6.
[97] In her "Commonplace Book," Brilliana had discussed the Lord's Supper.

"I found a sweetness in the service of God"

word "sweet" and its cognates, for example, provides an excellent window on her conviction in this regard. To open one's heart in prayer, for God's elect, is "a sweet thing."[98] Thus, she prayed for her son that he might "so … taste that sweetness in God's service which indeed is in it." "The men of this world cannot perceive it," she emphasized, for it is one of the choice blessings that accompanies the indwelling of the Spirit.[99] Indeed, she stressed, "the service of the Lord is more sweet, more peaceable, more delightful, than the enjoying of all the fading pleasures of the world."[100]

A concluding note

In the mid-1630s, one of Brilliana's siblings, her brother Edward (1594–1655), a loyal Royalist, wrote to Robert Harley that "in your house the order of things is inverted, you write to me of cheeses and my sister writes about a good scholar"![101] In a nutshell, this captures a key side of Brilliana's character, her vivacious intellectual curiosity. But, as this essay on her life and piety has sought to show, it was also a vivacity that was ultimately informed by a deep commitment to the Puritan vision of Christian godliness.

---

98   See Letters 8 and 16.
99   See Letter 5.
100 See Letter 19.
101 Cited Harris, "But I thinke and beleeve," 111.

Select letters of Lady Brilliana Harley

Letter 1[1]

October 5, 1627

Dear Sir:
Your two letters, one from Hereford and the other from Gloucester, were very welcome to me; and if you knew how gladly I receive your letters, I believe you would never let any opportunity pass. ...tomorrow I hope you will be well at your journey's end, where I wish myself to bid you welcome home. You see how my thoughts go with you; and as you have many of mine, so let me have some of yours. Believe me, I think I never missed you more than now I do, or else I have forgot what is past.[2] ...

I have sent you up a little hamper, in which is the box with the writings and books you bid me to send up, with the other things, sewed up in a cloth, in the bottom of the hamper. I have sent you a partridge pie, which has two pea chickens in it.[3] ...

I will now bid you good night, for it is past eleven o'clock. I pray God preserve you and give good success in all your business, and a speedy and happy meeting.

Your most faithful affectionate wife, Brilliana Harley.

---

[1] Brilliana Harley, Letter IV to Robert Harley in *Letters of the Lady Brilliana Harley*, 3.

[2] As noted in "An essay on the life and spirituality of Brilliana Harley," Brilliana frequently mentioned the depth of her love for her husband in her letters to him.

[3] By "pea chickens," Brilliana most likely meant peahens, which were commonly eaten by the wealthy well into the seventeenth century.

Letter 2[1]

December 4, 1629

My dear Sir:

I thank you for your letter, which I received this week by the carrier. ... Alas! my dear Sir, I know you do not to the one half of my desires, desire to see me, that loves you more than any earthly thing. I should be glad if you would but write me word, when I should hope to see you.

Ned has been ever since Sunday troubled with the rheum in his face very much.[2] ... The swelling of his face made him very dull; but now, I thank God, he is better, and begins to be merry. ... I must desire you to send me down a little Bible for him. He would not let me be in peace, till I promised him to send for one. He begins now to delight in reading; and that is the book I would have him place his delight in.

Tom has still a great cold; but he is not, I thank God, sick with it. Brill and Robin, I thank God, are well; and Brill has two teeth.[3] Ned presents his humble duty to you, and I beg your blessing for them all; and I beseech the Almighty to prosper you in all you do, and to give you a happy meeting with

Your most faithful affectionate wife, Brilliana Harley.

---

[1] Brilliana Harley, Letter VI to Robert Harley in *Letters of the Lady Brilliana Harley*, 4–5.

[2] Rheum is a watery discharge from the eyes or nose.

[3] The three children mentioned in this sentence are Thomas, Robert (or Robin) and Brilliana, whom Brilliana calls "Brill," a diminutive form that her own father Edward Conway had used for her. See *Manuscripts of His Grace the Duke of Portland*, III, 19.

Letter 3[1]

October 25, 1638

Good Ned:

I hope these lines will find you well at Oxford. I long to receive the assurance of your coming well to your journey's end. We have had fair weather since you went, and I hope it was so with you. ...

You are now in a place of more varieties than when you were at home; therefore take heed it take not up your thoughts so much as to neglect that constant service you owe to your God. When I lived abroad, I tasted something of those wiles;[2] therefore I may the more experimentally[3] give you warning. Remember me to your tutor, in whom I hope you will find daily more and more cause to love and respect.[4] I thank God my cold is something better than when you left me. I pray God bless you, and give you of those saving graces which will make you happy here and for ever hereafter.

Your most affectionate mother, Brilliana Harley.

---

[1] Brilliana Harley, Letter IX to Edward Harley in *Letters of the Lady Brilliana Harley*, 7.

[2] Brilliana had a similar view of the nation's capital: "London is a bewitching place" (Letter LXXXIV to Edward Harley, November 14, 1640, in *Letters of the Lady Brilliana Harley*, 101).

[3] i.e., experientially.

[4] Edward's Oxford tutor was Edward Perkins, who was a committed Puritan and Presbyterian. In 1640, for example, Perkins prayed in a letter to Edward Harley, "The Lord confound the bishops" (*Manuscripts of His Grace the Duke of Portland*, III, 68).

Puritan spirituality in the letters of Brilliana Harley

Magdalen Hall, University of Oxford

Letter 4[1]

November 2, 1638

Good Ned:
I was doubly glad to receive your letter, both for the assurance of your coming well to Oxford, and that I received it by your father's hand, who, I thank God, came well home yesterday, about four o'clock. I am glad you like Oxford; it is true it is to be liked, and happy are we, when we like both places and conditions that we must be in. If we could be so wise, we should find much more sweetness in our lives than we do: for certainly there is some good in all conditions (but that of sin), if we had the art to distract the sweet and leave the rest. Now I earnestly desire you may have that wisdom, that from all the flowers of learning you may draw the honey and leave the rest. ...

    I may well say, you are my well-beloved child; therefore, I cannot but tell you I miss you. I thank God I am something better with my cold than I was. ... Remember me to your tutor. If you would have anything, let me know it. Be not forgetful to write to me; and the Lord in mercy bless you, both with grace in your soul and the good things of this life.

    Your most affectionate mother till death, Brilliana Harley.

Be careful to keep the Sabbath.

---

[1] Brilliana Harley, Letter X to Edward Harley in *Letters of the Lady Brilliana Harley*, 8.

Licorice plants, from John Geard, *The Herball or General Historie of Plantes* with additions by Thomas Johnson (London: Adam Islip, Joice Norton, and Richard Whitakers, 1633), 1302.

Letter 5[1]

November 13, 1638

Good Ned

I beseech the Lord to bless you with those choice blessings of his Spirit, which none but his dear elect are partakers of; that so you may taste that sweetness in God's service which indeed is in it: but the men of this world cannot perceive it.

Think it not strange, if I tell you, I think it long since I heard from you; but my hope is that you are well, and my prayers are that you may be so. As you say you have found your tutor kind and careful of you, so I hope he will be so still. If you want anything, let me know it. ...

Your father, I thank God, is well; and for myself, I have not yet shaked off my cold. ... Your father prays God to bless you. Remember me to your tutor, and I beseech the Lord to keep you from all evil. I have sent you some juice of licorice, which you may keep to make use of, if you should have a cold.[2] So I rest,

Your most affectionate mother, Brilliana Harley.

---

[1] Brilliana Harley, Letter XI to Edward Harley in *Letters of the Lady Brilliana Harley*, 9.

[2] Licorice has been used since antiquity as an important herbal medicine for a variety of ailments, including respiratory conditions. With regard to the latter, it was used as an expectorant. See also Letter 9. For Brilliana's use of herbal medicine, see Henry Connor, "Lady Brilliana Harley (1598–1643): Her medicines and her doctors," *Journal of Medical Biography* 24, no.1 (2016): 128–130.

Letter 6[1]

November 17, 1638

Good Ned:

This day I received a letter from you, in which you write me, that you had written to me the week before; which letter I have not received, so that I thought it long since I heard from you. It is my joy that you are well, and I beseech the Lord to continue your health, and above all to give you that grace in your soul which may make you have a healthful soul, sound without errors, active in all that is good, industrious in all the ways in which good is to be gained.

I am glad you find a want of that ministry you did enjoy:[2] labour to keep a fresh desire after the sincere milk of the Word,[3] and then in good time you shall enjoy that blessing again. The Lord has promised to give his Spirit to his children, which shall lead them in the truth.[4] Beg that blessed Spirit, and then errors will but make the truth more bright, as the foil does a diamond.[5]

---

[1] Brilliana Harley, Letter XII to Edward Harley in *Letters of the Lady Brilliana Harley*, 9–11.

[2] This is an allusion to the fact that Laudian Arminians dominated the pulpits at Oxford. See Levy, "Perceptions and Beliefs," 169.

[3] Cf. a letter from her daughter Brilliana to Edward, January 25, 1638/39: "I am sorry that you have not the word of God, which I pray for, but I pray that God may guide by his Spirit that you may walk warily" (*Manuscripts of His Grace the Duke of Portland*, III, 54).

[4] Cf. John 16:13.

[5] "As the foil does a diamond" refers to the practice of placing a thin metallic or coloured foil behind a diamond to enhance its optical appearance.

My dear Ned, as you have been careful to choose your company, be so still, for pitch will not easily be touched without leaving some spot.[6] ...

I hope the news of the Swedes is not true;[7] but in all these things we must remember the warning, which our Saviour has given us, when he had told his disciples that there must be wars and rumours of wars.[8] But he saith, let not your hearts be troubled;[9] in my apprehension as if Christ had said, great troubles and wars must be, both to purge his Church of hypocrites, and that his enemies at the last may be utterly destroyed, but you, my servants, be not careful for yourselves, you are my jewels, and the days of trouble are the days when I take care of jewels. And, my dear Ned, tho[ough] I firmly believe there will be great troubles, yet I look with joy beyond those days of trouble, considering the glory that the Lord will bring his Church to; and happy are they that shall live to see it, which I hope you will do. ...

[S]ince I cannot speak with you, nor see you so often as I desire, I am willing to make these paper messengers my deputy. ...When you write by the carrier, write nothing but what any may see, for many times the letters miscarry. My dear Ned, you may see how willing I am to discourse with you, that have spun my letter out to this length. I thank God my

---

[6] Cf. a letter from her daughter Brilliana to Edward, February 15, 1638/39: "I am glad to hear that you do not love to keep company with those who fear not God" (*Manuscripts of His Grace the Duke of Portland*, III, 55).

[7] This is almost definitely a reference to Swedish support for Scotland during the months leading up to the First Bishops' War (1639). See Alexia Grosjean, *An Unofficial Alliance, Scotland and Sweden 1569–1654*, The Northern World, vol. 5 (Leiden; Boston: Brill, 2003), 165–190.

[8] Matthew 24:6.

[9] John 14:1a.

Letter 6

cold is gone. I beseech the Lord to bless you, as I desire my own soul should be blessed.

Your most affectionate mother, Brilliana Harley.

I have sent you a cake, which I hope you will eat in memory of Brampton.

Letter 7[1]

November 30, 1638

Good Ned:

... I give God thanks that you are recovered from that indisposition you felt, and thank you that you did send me word of it; for I desire to know how it is with you in all conditions. If you are ill, my knowing of it stirs me up more earnestly to pray for you. I believe that indisposition you felt was caused by some violent exercise. If you use to swinge,[2] let it not be violently, for exercise should be rather to refresh than tire nature. ...

Dear Ned, if I could as easily convey myself to you as my letters, I would not be so long absent from you; but, since I must wait for that comfort, I joy in this, that I assure myself, your prayers and mine meet daily at the throne of grace.

I must now tell you, your letter, by the carrier this week, was welcome to me; and your father has received his from you, and one from your tutor. I take it for a great blessing, that your worthy tutor gives so good a testimony of you, and that you esteem him so highly. I bless the Lord, that has given you favour in his eyes, to set his good will upon you. It is

---

[1] Brilliana Harley, Letter XIV to Edward Harley in *Letters of the Lady Brilliana Harley*, 13–14.

[2] This is a curious use of "swinge." Did Brilliana use it to mean "to whirl around"? So, did she have in mind, her son whirling his body around in exercise? Or did she use the verb with the meaning "to beat, flog, thrash"? If so, was she thinking of Ned beating his body up in exercise? Or again, did she employ the verb as a variant of "to singe, scorch"? In which case, did she envisage her son working up a sweat in exercise? For help with thinking through the possible usages, I am indebted to Prof. John Coffey.

found experimentally true that conquerors must be as careful to keep what they have gained as they were to obtained it. It is alike true, we must be, as careful and studious to keep good opinions and affections toward us as we were to gain them; and I hope you will be a good practitioner of that lesson.

Dear Ned, if you would have anything, send me word; or if I thought a cold pie, or such a thing, would be of any pleasure to you, I would send it to you. But your father says you care not for it, and Mrs. Pierson[3] tells me, when her son was at Oxford, and she sent him such things, he prayed her that she would not.

I thank you for *The Man in the Moone*.[4] I had heard of the

---

3 This is undoubtedly Helen Pierson, the widow of Thomas Pierson (d.1633), the moderate Puritan rector of Brampton Bryan from 1612 until his death. Robert Harley had brought Pierson to Brampton Bryan so that he might take an active role in evangelizing the area around Brampton Bryan in Herefordshire, Shropshire and Radnorshire. For Helen Pierson, see Letter 12. For Thomas Pierson, see Jacqueline Eales, "Thomas Pierson and the Transmission of the Moderate Puritan Tradition," *Midland History*, 20:1 (1995): 75–102. Eales notes his dynamic evangelism around Brampton Bryan on page 97 of her article. See also Susan Levy, "Perceptions and Beliefs: The Harleys of Brampton Bryan and the Origins and Outbreak of the English Civil War" (PhD thesis, London University, 1983), 148–150.

4 The reference here is to *The man in the Moone: or, A Discourse of a Voyage thither by Domingo Gonsales The Speedy Messenger* (London: John Norton, 1638), which was written by Francis Godwin, the Bishop of Hereford, and published posthumously and anonymously in 1638 (a second edition in 1657 identified Godwin by his initials). The frontispiece depicts the method by which the purported author of the book, a Spaniard by the name of Domingo Gonsales, was able to fly to the moon in eleven or twelve days. He discovered a type of wild swan, called a gansas, a number of which bore him to the moon. Once on the moon, he came across its inhabitants whose clothes were "neither black, nor white, yellow, nor red, green nor blue, nor any colour composed of these. ... it was a colour never seen in our earthly world, and therefore neither to be described unto us by any, nor to be conceived of one that never saw it. For as it were a hard matter to describe unto a man born blind the difference between blue and green, so can I not bethink my self any means how to decipher unto you this Lunar colour, having no affinity with any other that ever I beheld with mine eyes. Only this I can say of it, that it was the most glorious and delightful, that can possibly be imagined; neither in truth was there any one thing, that more delighted me, during my

Title-page of Francis Godwin's *The Man in the Moone* (1638)

---

abode in that new world, then the beholding of that most pleasing and resplendent colour" (71–72). So gorgeous is this colour, Domingo was confident that a person would "travel 1000 Leagues to behold it" (99).

When Domingo first met the inhabitants, he, being stuck with amazement, crossed himself and "cried out Iesus Maria." At the name of Jesus, the inhabitants "young and old, fell all down upon their knees" (72–73). The moon, it turns out, is a sort of paradise, a place of "perpetual Spring" with neither theft nor murder nor sexual immorality (102–104), though the inhabitants do "make continual use of Tobacco" (109, 105).

Godwin's book was written at a time of great astronomical interest in the moon and the possibility that it was inhabited. Diane Purkiss notes that Brilliana's interest in this novel "shows that she was herself an adventurous and curious reader" (*The English Civil War: A Peoples' History* [London: HarperCollins, 2006], 149).

book, but not seen it; by as much as I have looke[d] upon [it], I find it some [a]kin to *Don Quixote*.[5] I would willingly have the French book you write me word of; but if it can be had, I desire it in French, for I had rather anything in that tongue than in English. I know not certainly whether I have it, till I see it. ...

Dear Ned, the Lord in heaven bless you, and give you that principle of grace, which may never die in you, but that you may grow in grace, and so have the favour of your God, which is better than life, and the favour of good men, which small number is worth all the millions of men besides. So, assuring you that I still rejoice to show myself

Your most affectionate mother till death, Brilliana Harley.

I wrote to [you] the last week; send me word whether you had my letter; I would not have it lost.
In haste.

---

5 The famous novel by Miguel de Cervantes (1547–1616). Harley spelled it "Donqueshot."

Letter 8[1]

December 11, 1638

Good Ned:

… I take it for a great mercy of God, that you have your health; the Lord in mercy continue it to you, and be you careful of yourself. The means to preserve health is a good diet and exercise: and, as I hope you are not wanting in your care for your health, so I hope you are much more careful for your soul, that that better part of yours may grow in the ways of knowledge. And in some proportion, it is with the soul as with the body; there must be a good diet; we must feed upon the Word of God, which when we have done we must not let it lie idle, but we must be diligent in exercising of what we know, and the more we practice the more we shall know.

Dear Ned, let nothing hinder you from performing constant private duties of praying and reading. Experimentally,[2] I may say that private prayer is one of the best means to keep the heart close to God. O it is a sweet thing to open our hearts to our God, as to a friend. If it had not been for that I had recourse to my God sure I should have fainted before this. …

---

[1] Brilliana Harley, Letter XV to Edward Harley in *Letters of the Lady Brilliana Harley*, 14–15.

[2] i.e., experientially.

The Ember week[3] now draws on apace. I wish you and your tutor were here then. Howsoever I hope, you will in desires be with us; and so our prayers, I hope, shall meet in heaven, before the Lord. I beseech the Lord to bless you, and that you may be still the beloved child of

Your most affectionate mother, Brilliana Harley.

... *In haste after supper.*

---

3 According to the liturgical calendar of Western Christian churches, there are four Ember weeks in the year: the weeks following Holy Cross Day (September 14), the Feast of St Lucy (December 13), the first Sunday in Lent and Pentecost. Harley must then be referring to the December Ember week. These weeks involve periods of prayer, fasting and abstinence.

Letter 9[1]

December 14, 1638

Good Ned:

... My dear Ned, be still watchful over yourself, that custom in seeing and hearing of vice do not abate your distaste for it. I bless my God, for those good desires you have, and the comfort you find in serving your God. Be confident, he is the best Master, and will give the best wages, and they wear the best livery, the garment of holiness, a clothing which shall never wear out, but is renewed every day. I remember you in my prayers, as I do my own soul, for you are as dear to me as my life. I hope in a special manner, we shall remember you at the fast;[2] and, dear Ned, think upon that day, how your father

---

[1] Brilliana Harley, Letter XVI to Edward Harley in *Letters of the Lady Brilliana Harley*, 16–17.

[2] See Letter 8 and note 3. Fasting was a significant feature in Puritanism and in the Harley household. See Patrick Collinson, "Lectures by Combination: Structures and Characteristics of Church Life in 17th-Century England," *Bulletin of the Institute of Historical Research* 48 (1975): 189–190; Gareth Townley, "What do the religious beliefs of the Harleys of Brampton Bryan, Herefordshire, tell us about the nature of early Stuart puritanism?" (MA thesis, Durham University, 2016), 57–59; and Fiona Ann Counsell, "Domestic Religion in Seventeenth Century English Gentry Households" (PhD thesis, University of Birmingham, 2017), 221–243. Counsell deals with fasting in the Harley household (233–239). As Counsell notes: "The Harleys family fast practices played a vital role in constructing and consolidating their family religious identity as members of the godly community" (236). See also Levy, "Perceptions and Beliefs," 152–155.

For a reflection on the nature of fasting by a Presbyterian pastor close to the Harleys, namely, John Greene of Pencombe, Herefordshire, see his *Nehemiah's Teares and Prayers for Judah's Affliction, And the ruines and repaire*

Seneca (4 BC–AD 65)

Letter 9

is used to spend it, that so you may have like affections to join with us. Let your desire be oftener presented before God that day; and the Lord, who only hears prayers, hear us all.

Dear Ned, be careful to use exercise; and for that pain in your back, it may be caused by some indisposition of the kidneys. I would have you drink in the morning beer boiled with licorice; it is a most excellent thing for the kidneys.

For the book, if you cannot have it in French, send it me in English; and I will, if please God, send you money for it.

Dear Ned, it is very well done, that you submit to your father's desire in your clothes; and that is a happy temper, both to be contented with plain clothes and in the wearing of better clothes, not to think oneself the better for them, nor to be troubled if you be in plain clothes, and see others of your rank in better. Seneca[3] had not got that victory over himself; for in his country house he lived privately, yet he complains that when he came to court, he found a tickling desire to [be] like them at court. ...

The Lord in much mercy bless you, and preserve you from all evil, especially that of sin; and so I rest

Your most affectionate mother, Brilliana Harley.

---

of Jerusalem (London: Philemon Stephens, 1644), 24–25. Greene had preached this sermon before the House of Commons, and Robert Harley encouraged Greene, on behalf of the House, to have it printed (*Die Mercurii*, April 24, 1644; frontispiece to Greene, *Nehemiah's Teares and Prayers*).

3 Here Brilliana used the French rendering of the name of Seneca (4 BC–AD 65), Seneque, but without any accents. She referred again to Seneca when she had occasion to comment on the execution of Thomas Wentworth (1593–1641), the 1st Earl of Strafford: he "died like a Seneca, but not like one that had tasted the mystery of godliness" (Letter CXVIII to Edward Harley, May 21, 1641, in *Letters of the Lady Brilliana Harley*, 131).

Letter 10[1]

January 4, 1638/39

My good Ned:
… nothing here below on the earth is more dear to me, than your well being. It is that, I pray for, and rejoice when I am assured of it; but my dear Ned, above all, the well being of your soul is most dear to me, next to my own. I rejoice, that you keep that acquaintance with yourself, as to take notice of the passages on your heart. Keep that watch still, and the more you know of yourself, the less will you trust in yourself, and then you will desire to be set in that Rock, which is higher than yourself, and so you will be safe.[2]

… I hope … you will keep to the truth in everything; and, in my opinion, he who stands for the truth in small things (as we think, for none of God's truths in his service is small), is of a more courageous spirit, than on that day [those who] will only shew themselves in great matters. I hope this letter will meet you returned safe to the university, which I should be glad to be assured of. My dear Ned, write to me as soon as you can; for I long to hear from you, and the Lord in mercy let me hear well from you.

… The Lord in mercy bless you, and give you a heart to understand those things which belong to your peace, both in this life and your everlasting peace; and the Lord preserve

---

[1] Brilliana Harley, Letter XVII to Edward Harley in *Letters of the Lady Brilliana Harley*, 17–18.

[2] An allusion to Psalm 61:2–3.

your health, and prosper your endeavours in the ways of knowledge; and still believe, that I take comfort in expressing myself

Your most affectionate mother, Brilliana Harley.

... Mr. Gower [3] *tells me, he wrote to you, and so did I, by the carrier of Leominster, when your father wrote to your tutor; for your father wrote by both the carriers, fearing the one of them might fail the delivery of his letter.*

---

3 Stanley Gower (1600–1660) succeeded Thomas Pierson as the rector of Brampton Bryan. He was a Presbyterian in his ecclesial convictions and served as one of the divines at the Westminster Assembly in the 1640s. He was critical of the education at both Oxford and Cambridge universities. In his words, "I am sure the fountain of our impieties lies in the Universities" (Letter to Sir Robert Harley, January 2, 1641, in *Manuscripts of His Grace the Duke of Portland*, III, 71). He was regarded by the Royalists in Herefordshire as "a mover of sedition" (Brilliana Harley, Letter CVI to Edward Harley, March 25, [1642,] in *Letters of the Lady Brilliana Harley*, 121). For the date of this letter, see Lewis, "Introduction" to *Letters of the Lady Brilliana Harley*, xiv.

He also had little love for the Independents, i.e., Congregationalists, and the Baptists, but they could be equally critical of Gower. According to young Thomas Harley, the Welsh Congregationalist Walter Cradock once described Gower as "a base, filthy fellow and a drunkard," and "that he never preached anything worth a pin" (Letter to Edward Harley, January 29, 1641, in *Manuscripts of His Grace the Duke of Portland*, III, 73). On the other hand, Brilliana had certain concerns with Cradock. See Letter 15. Also see Levy, "Perceptions and Beliefs," 170.

On Gower, see Jacqueline Eales, *Puritans and Roundheads: The Harleys of Brampton Bryan and the Outbreak of the English Civil War* (Cambridge: Cambridge University Press, 1990), 56–57; Diane Purkiss, *The English Civil War: A People's History* (London: HarperCollins, 2006), 145.

Letter 11[1]

January 14, 1638/39

My good Ned:
I think it long since I heard from you, but my hope is that you are well. My thoughts are as much upon you now, as when you were with me, and therefore I must conclude, that absence abates no love, but that which is but a shadow of love. ... the Lord in mercy fill you with his grace, that so you may be lovely in his sight; and if you are beloved by the Lord, it is happiness enough. None are partakers of his love but his children; and he so loved them, that he gave his Son to die for them. O that we could but see the depth of that love of God in Christ to us: then sure, love would constrain us to serve the Lord, with all our hearts most willingly.

And this love of the Lord is not common to all. Others may partake of his mercy, as Ahab, who the Lord spared upon his humiliation;[2] and they may partake of his power, as the King in Samaria did, when the Lord made plenty to flow in the city, after so great a famine.[3] And all his creatures partake of his liberality in feeding them, and his most wise government of the things here below; but none tastes of his love but his chosen ones; and if we be loved of the Lord, what need

---

[1] Brilliana Harley, Letter XVIII to Edward Harley in *Letters of the Lady Brilliana Harley*, 19–20.

[2] For the biblical account of Ahab, king of the northern kingdom of Israel, see 1 Kings 16:29–22:40.

[3] For this event, see 2 Kings 6:24–7:20.

Puritan spirituality in the letters of Brilliana Harley

John Calvin (1509–1564)

we care what the men of the world think of us? We in that respect, should be like a good wife, who cares not, how ill favoured all men else think her, if her husband love her.

And, my dear Ned, as this love of the Lord is his peculiar gift, only to his dear ones, let it be your chief care to get assurance of that love of God in Christ; and, since he has loved you, show your love to him, by hating that which he hates, which is sin; and it was sin that crucified our Lord, that so loved us that he gave himself for us.[4] …

Be constant in holy duties; let public and private go together. Let not the one shove out the other. I believe, before this, you have read some part of Mr. Calvin; send me word how you like him.[5] I have sent you a little purse with some small money in it, all the pence I had, … that you may sometimes remember her, that seldom has you out of my thoughts. The Lord bless you.

Your most affectionate mother, Brilliana Harley.

I have sent your tutor a small token. I cannot but desire to show thanks to him, who shows so much love to you. I here enclosed send you the bookbinders' letter from Worcester, that you may see books are not so cheap as in Oxford.

---

4 Cf. Ephesians 5:2.
5 It bears noting that Brilliana could be critical of Calvin. See Letter 28.

John Scudamore (1601–1671)

Letter 12[1]

January 19, 1638/39

Dear Ned:
I pray God bless you, first with those rich graces of his Spirit, and then with the good things of this life. ... I may well say, that my life is bound with yours, and I hope I shall never have cause to recall or repent of my love, with which I love you.

... Mr Scudamore,[2] that dwells hard by Hereford, ... told your father the other day at Hereford, that he would see you at Oxford. He has been abroad in France and Italy. If he do come to you, be careful to use him with all respect.[3]

But in the entertaining of any such, be not put out of yourself; speak freely, and always remember, that they are but men; and for being gentlemen, it puts no distance between you; for you have part in nobleness of birth. Tho[ugh] some

---

[1] Brilliana Harley, Letter XIX to Edward Harley in *Letters of the Lady Brilliana Harley*, 21–22.

[2] John Scudamore (1601–1671) of Holme Lacy, was a friend of William Laud. He was a diplomat and politician who had studied at Magdalen Hall, where Edward Harley was studying. Between 1635 and 1639, he was the English ambassador to France. Firmly convinced of episcopal church government—when he was in France, he refused to attend worship at non-episcopal Huguenot temples—he took the Royalist side during the Civil War and aided the Royalists in their siege of Brampton Bryan. See the account of the siege in "Brampton Bryan" in *Calendar of the Manuscripts*, I, 6–7, and the letters between Brilliana and Scudamore in *Calendar of the Manuscripts*, I, 14–22. For an examination of his career, see Ian Atherton, *Ambition and Failure in Stuart England: The Career of John, First Viscount Scudamore* (Manchester: Manchester University Press, 1999). For his religious views, see especially Chapter 3. Brilliana rendered his name "Scidamore."

[3] i.e., treat him with all respect.

have place before you, yet you may be in their company. And this I say to you, not to make you proud or conceited of yourself, but that you should know yourself, and so not to be put out of yourself, when you are in better company than ordinary. For I have seen many, when they come into good company, lose themselves. Surely, they have too high esteem of man; for they can go boldly to God, and lose themselves before men. Remember, therefore, when you are with them, that you are but with those who are such as yourself; th[ough] some, wiser and more honourable.

... Mrs. Pierson[4] is still ill, I pray God spare her, if it be his will.

---

4 i.e., Helen Pierson. See Letter 7.

Letter 13[1]

[no date]

Good Ned:

... I think it well that your tutor has made you handsome clothes, and I desire you should go handsomely.

... Dear Ned, I am exceeding glad that you did set Wednesday apart.[2] I hope the Lord did hear us all; and now our duty is, when we have so prayed, and so promised, to be more watchful and obedient to our God, that we do not turn again to folly, and like broken bows that start aside,[3] for so we shall lose our pains, and the sweet fruit of our prayers, and bring more sorrow upon our souls.

Dear Ned, I thank you for joining with me in desiring I might be able to go to the congregation and the beauty of holiness. It is true, my sweet Ned, I may truly say, one thing I have desired, and that I will seek after, that I might enjoy those sweet privileges in God's house;[4] but since you went I have not had that happiness. The sharpness of the weather is such as I cannot bear it so long together. I must wait under the gracious hand of my God.

... And now, my dear Ned, in company and in enjoying the recreations of this life, look to your heart, that you may

---

[1] Brilliana Harley, Letter XX to Edward Harley in *Letters of the Lady Brilliana Harley*, 22–23.

[2] A reference to a day of fasting and prayer.

[3] "To start aside" here has the meaning of deviating or swerving from a straight path. The simile then is of a broken bow that cannot shoot straight.

[4] A reference to Psalm 27.

reserve a higher measure of joy and delight for the service of your God; and to do so, labour to find out the vanity in all the things here below. The vanity is this, they last not; and there is a weariness in them, if they be still enjoyed. The Lord bless you.

Letter 14[1]

January 26, 1638/39

Good Ned:

... The Lord in mercy continue your health, and, above, the Lord in his rich mercy give you such life in Christ, that you may have a strong and lively soul, always active in the ways of grace.

My dear Ned, be careful of yourself, and forget not. Do exercise; for health can no more be had without it, than without a good diet. I much rejoice, and give the Lord thanks, that Mr. Perkins[2] was an instrument to bring two in my dear brother's family out of darkness into light, and from the power of sin, under the sweet regiment of our Lord Christ Jesus. I am confident, your worthy tutor rejoices in it, that he did so shine as to bring glory to his Lord and Master; and as the work is begun, and we rejoice in it, so I desire from my soul, that the Lord would perfect it.

I begun with this, because I most rejoice in it; and now I must tell you, I am glad my brother's house is so well governed, and that his daughter and son are of so good dispositions. I pray God, add grace to it, and then it will be a sweet harmony. I am not sorry that everyone tells you, you are like my lord. I have not been very well these three days, and so enforced me to keep my bed, as I have done many times,

---

[1] Brilliana Harley, Letter XXI to Edward Harley in *Letters of the Lady Brilliana Harley*, 23–24.

[2] i.e., Edward Perkins. See Letter 3.

when you were with me. I hope, I shall be able to rise today. My letter should have been longer, had not I been in bed. ...

Dear Ned: My age is no secret. ... When I was married to your father, your father would have been asked in the church, but my lord would by no means consent; what his reason was, I know not. Then they have a custom, that, when they fetch out the license, the age of the woman must be known; so that, if I would have hidden my age, then it must be known, and then I was between two or three and twenty. I was not full three and twenty, but in the license they wrote me three and twenty, and you know how long I have been married, for you know how old you are, and you were born when I had been married a year and 3 months.

Letter 15[1]

February 1, 1638/39

Good Ned:

... Mr Cradock is a worthy man, but sometimes he does not judge clearly of things, and when we meet with such men, we must look through the cloud of their infirmities upon the sunshine of their virtues.[2]

... You long since [have] written for Sir Walter Raleigh's *History*[3] to your father. I did not forget it, and have sent it you by this carrier, with a book of news. I would have sent you the relation of the taking of Brisake, which is of great importance, but your father left it at the bishop's.[4]

---

[1] Brilliana Harley, Letter XXII to Edward Harley in *Letters of the Lady Brilliana Harley*, 25–27.

[2] On Walter Cradock, see "An essay on the life and spirituality of Brilliana Harley."

[3] Walter Raleigh (c.1553–1618), *The History of the World* (London: Walter Burre, 1617). There were numerous editions of Raleigh's work in the seventeenth century.

[4] Brilliana is referring to news about the siege of Breisach, in the Rhine Valley, in Baden-Württemberg, which was taken by the French in December 1638 after a four-month siege. This military action was part of the Thirty Years' War.

There were some in Brilliana's day who regarded news as "a distraction from less time-bound verities" (Joad Raymond, *Pamphlets and Pamphleteering in Early Modern Britain* [Cambridge: Cambridge University Press, 2003], 98). The Yorkshire Puritan John Shawe (1608–1672) thus considered it to be a sign of godliness that his first wife, Dorothy Heathcote (d.1657), had no interest in news outside of what concerned the church and the progress of the Christian faith (*Mistris Shawe's Tomb-stone. Or, The Saints Remains* [London: Nathanael Brooks, 1658], 17). On the other hand, Brilliana, as this passage clearly reveals, "saw no conflict between her religion, news pamphlets, and

Walter Raleigh (c.1553–1618)

Letter 15

I have sent you another little book;[5] you saw me have it, when you were with me. I have read it, and it pleases me better then anything I have read [in] a long time, and anything that is good, which I enjoy, especially in the best things. ...

Dear Ned, read it, at your leisure, and well weigh it, and then let me know how you like it; for my part I am much in love with it.

... and till your father keeps his promises, in giving you a watch, I will let you have mine; but I will not venture it by the carrier. ...

---

more scholarly pursuits" (Raymond, *Pamphlets and Pamphleteering*, 98). For Brilliana's view of news, see also Letters 18 and 23.

5 Brilliana does not identify the title of this book.

Letter 16[1]

February 2, 1638/39

Good Ned:

… I beseech the Lord to bless you, with those choice blessings, with which I desire my own soul should be blessed with. My dear Ned, be watchful that you grow not slack in keeping the sabbath, and in the performing of private duties. O it is a sweet thing to have private conference with our God, to whom we may make known all our wants, all our follies, and discover all our weaknesses, in assurance that he will supply our wants, and will not upbraid us with our infirmities. …

---

[1] Brilliana Harley, Letter XXIII to Edward Harley in *Letters of the Lady Brilliana Harley*, 28.

Letter 17[1]

February 8, 1638/39

Good Ned:
It is my great comfort, that you enjoy your health, which I was assured of this day by your letter. It is my greater joy that you thirst after the sweet waters of God's Word in a powerful ministry. I hope the Lord will grant you, your desire in that kind.

Dear Ned, labour to keep up the life of your soul and be earnest with God, to bless the small means you have, that by his blessing, a little may do you much good, and that his Spirit may heat the coldness of it. ... As I wrote to you, I thank God, we kept Wednesday last,[2] and I bless God, I joined with them, and so did your sister Brill and brothers. If ever we had cause to pray, it is now. Sure the Lord is about a glorious work. He is refining his church; and happy will those days be, when she comes out like gold. And if ever wicked men had cause to fear, it is now; for certainly the Lord will call them to account. Their day is at hand. Let us be found mourners, that so we may be marked.

I thank God, I am now out of my chamber again. Your father is well and so is your brother Robert. ... The rest are

---

[1] Brilliana Harley, Letter XXIV to Edward Harley in *Letters of the Lady Brilliana Harley*, 28–29.

[2] Brilliana is referring to keeping the previous Wednesday as a day of fasting and prayer.

well. Mrs. Pierson[3] is so well, that she goes abroad. ...

For that from abroad, I refer you to this enclosed printed book. I purpose, if please God, to remember you with some of Brampton diet, against Lent.[4] I wish you may not eat too much fish. I know you like it; but I think it is not so good for you.

---

3 i.e., Helen Pierson. See Letters 7 and 12.
4 The use of the term "against" here has the sense of "in preparation for."

Letter 18[1]

March 1, 1638/39

Good Ned:

I beseech the Lord to bless you, with those choice blessings, which are only the portion of his elect; in which the men of this life, have no part. They are hid from their eyes. Only in the day of trouble and death, then they know there is a happiness belonging to God's children, which they would then partake of, and howl, for the want of that comfort. ...

Dear Ned, do not let your diet be, this Lent, all together fish.[2] I am well pleased, if the pies fitted your taste, and your friends'.[3] ...

There is a book, which is written by a Papist that is converted; it discovers much; I would, if I could, have gained it and have sent you the book.[4] ...

I have sent you a book of news. ... I would willingly have your mind keep awake in the knowledge of things abroad.

---

[1] Brilliana Harley, Letter XXVI to Edward Harley in *Letters of the Lady Brilliana Harley*, 31–32.

[2] Cf. Brilliana Harley, Letter LXVI to Edward Harley, February 28, 1639/40, in *Letters of the Lady Brilliana Harley*, 83: "I hope you will find out some way not to keep a strict Lent, for I am confident is not good for you."; idem, Letter LXVIII to Edward Harley, March 14, 1639/40, in *Letters of the Lady Brilliana Harley*, 85: "I hope you are careful not to eat too much fish this Lent."

[3] On February 15, Brilliana informed her son that she had sent him "a turkey pie and 6 pies" (Brilliana Harley, Letter XXV to Edward Harley in *Letters of the Lady Brilliana Harley*, 30–31).

[4] Brilliana does not specify the title of this book.

Letter 19[1]

March 22, 1638/39

My good Ned:

The last week being not well, I could not enjoy this contentment of writing to you. You may remember, that when you were at home, I was often enforced to keep my bed; it pleases God, it is so with me still, and when I have those indispositions it makes me ill for some time afterward. It is the hand of my gracious God; and tho[ugh] it be sharp, yet when I look at the will of God in it, it is sweetened to me: for to me, there is nothing can sweeten any condition to us, in this life, but as we look at God in it, and see ourselves his servants in that condition in which we are.

Therefore. when I consider my own afflictions, they are not so bitter, when I look at the will of my God in it. He is pleased it should be so, and then, should not I be pleased it should be so? And I hope, the Lord will give me a heart still to wait upon my God; and I hope the Lord will look graciously upon me.

And my dearest, believe this from me, that there is no sweetness in any thing in this life to be compared to the sweetness in the service of our God, and this I thank God, I can say, not only to agree with those that say so, but experimentally.[2] I

---

[1] Brilliana Harley, Letter XXVIII to Edward Harley in *Letters of the Lady Brilliana Harley*, 33–35.

[2] Cf. Brilliana Harley, Letter LVI to Edward Harley, November 25, 1639, in *Letters of the Lady Brilliana Harley*, 74: "O! sweet is the service of our God, that gives sweetness in the midst of bitterness."

have had health and friends and company in variety, and there was a time, that what could I have said I wanted; yet in all that there was a trouble, and that which gave me peace, was serving of my God, and not the service of the world.

And I have had a time of sickness, and weakness, and the loss of friends, and as I may say, the gliding away of all those things I took most comfort in, in this life. If I should now say (which I may boldly) that, in this condition, O how sweet did I find the love of my God, and the endeavour, to walk in his ways; it may be, some may say, then it must needs be so, because all my other comforts failed me. But my dear Ned I must lay both my conditions together; my time of freedom from afflictions, and my time of afflictions; and in the one, I found a sweetness in the service of God, above the sweetness of the things in this life, and in trouble a sweetness in the service of God, which took away the bitterness of the affliction; and this I tell you, that you may believe how good the Lord is, and believe it, as a tried truth, the service of the Lord is more sweet, more peaceable, more delightful, than the enjoying of all the fading pleasures of the world.

Letter 20[1]

March 29, 1639

Dear Ned:

I am sorry your eyes have been sore, and glad I am that you found benefits by what Mr. Wilkinson[2] gave you. ... I have sent you a glass of eye water, which is not only good to cure sore eyes but to preserve the eyes' sight. Drop a little of the water into your eyes, in the morning and at night. But I hope this water will come to your hands when your eyes are well.[3] Tho[ough] I am not afraid of[4] your eyes, yet I cannot but pity you[5] them; for by experience, I know it to be a great pain. For once I had sore eyes, and when by experience we feel how tender the eye is, we may call to mind, how sensible God is of all the wrongs which are done his children, when he is pleased to say, that they which touch his children, touch the apple of his eye.[6] Therefore woe be to those that are so bold; and happy are those that are in that account with the Lord.

---

[1] Brilliana Harley, Letter XXIX to Edward Harley in *Letters of the Lady Brilliana Harley*, 36–37.

[2] John Wilkinson (1588–1650) was principal of Magdalen Hall from 1605 to 1643.

[3] It was not until the autumn of this year that Edward informed his mother that his eyes were finally fine. See Brilliana Harley, Letter L to Edward Harley, October 24, 1639, in *Letters of the Lady Brilliana Harley*, 66.

[4] Brilliana uses the preposition "of" here with the meaning "concerning, about; with regard to, regarding."

[5] Brilliana writes "your," but must mean "you."

[6] See Zechariah 2:8.

My dear Ned, I long to see you, and I trust the Lord will give me that comfort. I thank God the Lord vouchsafed me, that privily on the last Lord's Day, that I was partaker of the comfort in his public ordinance.[7] Mr. Gower did not preach, but Mr. Blinman did, who preached very well.[8] He says he knows you, and he commends Mr. Perkins[9] very much, which I am very glad to hear so large a commendation as he gives. He is now without a place, being lately put out of one.

... I thank God, I took no hurt in going to church; a little cold I have, but I hope it will wear away. I ride one day abroad.

---

[7] Cf. Brilliana Harley, Letter CXXIX to Edward Harley, July 23, 1641, in *Letters of the Lady Brilliana Harley*, 141–142: "I pray God in mercy, if it be his holy will, make me partaker of those sweet privileges of his public ordinances." Cf. also a rare reference to the Lord's Supper in Brilliana Harley, Letter CXLII to Edward Harley, undated, in *Letters of the Lady Brilliana Harley*, 151: "Tomorrow there is a sacrament, and I hope to be at it."

[8] On Stanley Gower, see Letter 10. On Richard Blinman's (1609–c.1681) career, see "Richard Blinman (bef. 1609–bef. 1681)" (https://www.wikitree.com/wiki/Blinman-1#Will.3B_Death.3B_Estate; accessed June 30, 2024). At the time of this letter, as Brilliana went on to observe, Blinman did not have a pastorate and he was preaching at various locales along the English-Welsh border. In the early months of 1640, he decided to emigrate to New England. Brilliana referred to this when she stated in a letter to Ned: "Mr Blinman is gone into New England" (February 28, 1639/40 [*Letters of the Lady Brilliana Harley*, 84]). Given the fact that voyages to New England were generally not made in the winter months, the phrase "is gone" is best understood as "is going" rather than "has gone." See "Richard Blinman (bef. 1609–bef. 1681)."

[9] Ned's tutor at Oxford. See Letter 3.

Letter 21[1]

April 5, 1639

Dear Ned:
There is no earthly thing that is of more comfort to me than your being well. Therefore, you may easily believe your letters are sweet comforts to me, and so was your letter this week. I bless my God that you have your health, and the Lord in mercy continue that comfort to you and me. My dear Ned, I should be exceeding glad, if your tutor would be willing to let you come home at Whitsuntide. If he will but say the word, I believe all parties would agree; … for I desire, if please the Lord, to have you at home the long vacation as they call it. My dear Ned, let me know your mind, whether you are willing, and whether your tutor be so too, but so that he will be pleased to spend some time with us at Brampton.

As they do at Oxford, so they do in all places, take liberty to inveigh against Puritans.[2] We hear the Scots have taken possession of the King's house in Edinburgh.[3] Sure this summer is likely to produce great matters. The Lord show mercy upon his poor servants. …

---

[1] Brilliana Harley, Letter XXXI to Edward Harley to Edward Harley in *Letters of the Lady Brilliana Harley*, 39–41.

[2] On the embrace of the term "Puritan" by Robert Harley, see "An essay on the life and spirituality of Brilliana Harley."

[3] In March 1639, during the First Bishop's War, when Charles I sought to impose episcopacy upon the Church of Scotland, Edinburgh was seized by the Scottish Covenanters.

I have told you if you remember of a paper that some statesmen make use of, when they would not have known what they write of. Write me word whether you understand what I mean.[4] ...

I thank you for the book you sent, but yet I nor your father have not read any of it.

---

4 Brilliana is referring to a technique known as the grille cipher that had been employed since the previous century to create coded letters. The grille was a perforated sheet, often made of cardboard, as the vehicle of encryption. To encode a message, the writer placed the perforated sheet over a blank piece of paper and wrote the secret message through the holes. After the message had been put in place, the sender then filled in the gaps with other words that hid the message and provided an innocuous-sounding letter. The recipient, possessing the identical grille, placed it over the encrypted letter to reveal the message. For further details, see David Kahn, *The Codebreakers: The Story of Secret Writing* (New York: The Macmillan Co., 1967), 144–145. For copies of some of the encrypted letters, see *Letters of the Lady Brilliana Harley*, 191–194, 196–199.

Letter 22[1]

April 16, 1639

Dear Ned:

... I beseech the Lord to bless you, and to fill your soul with those sweet graces of his Spirit, by which you may both know and taste the goodness of the Lord. The Lord is good, and good to his, and his "service is perfect freedom";[2] and happy are they that are of his family, who serve him daily, and not as a retainer.

My dear Ned, be still watchful over your heart, that nothing steal away your affections from your God, who alone has loved us and who alone is to be believed. ...

I have not been well these 4 days, being extremely troubled with a beating at my heart. I thank God, this day I have been something better than I was since Thursday. I hope the Lord will be merciful to me in all conditions. ...

I thank you for the books you sent me: the 2 speeches against the Scots. I read them both; they both show of what spirit they are. ...

Strangers are in the parlour, and there I must end this discourse, to discourse with them, but I am well pleased when I can express myself.

---

[1] Brilliana Harley, Letter XXXIII to Edward Harley in *Letters of the Lady Brilliana Harley*, 42–43.

[2] The phrase "whose service is perfect freedom" is found in "A Collect for Peace" at the close of the order of worship for morning prayer in *The Book of Common Prayer*, which Brilliana knew well. She used this expression again in Letter XXXVIII to Edward Harley, undated (*Letters of the Lady Brilliana Harley*, 48).

Letter 23[1]

May 7, 1639

Dear Ned:

… I like the stuff for your clothes well; but the colour[2] of those for every day I do not like so well; but the silk chamlet[3] I like very well, both colour and stuff. Let your stockings[4] be always of the same colour of your clothes, and I hope you now wear Spanish leather shoes. If your tutor does not intend to buy you silk stockings to wear with your silk shirt, send me word, and I will, if please God, bestow a pair on you. …

I thank God, your father is well, and on Thursday next he goes, if please God, to Hereford. For myself, I have not been very well; but this day, I thank God, I have been something better. I have been a long time in the school of affliction, where I desire not to be wary of the correction of my heavenly Father, but to learn obedience under it.

Here enclosed I have sent you some foreign news, being still desirous to have your mind keep awake in the consideration of the affairs abroad. I thank you for the King's book.

---

[1] Brilliana Harley, Letter XXXIX to Edward Harley in *Letters of the Lady Brilliana Harley*, 50–51.
[2] Here Harley spelt this word "cullor." In the very next sentence, she spelled it "culler."
[3] A chamlet, also referred to as camelot, or camblet, was a woven fabric made from wool and silk.
[4] Harley spelled this word "stokens."

Martin Luther (1483–1546)

Letter 24[1]

May 10, 1639

Dear Ned:

... Having been often not well, and confined to so solitary a place as my bed, I made choice of an entertainment for myself, which might be easy and of some benefit to myself; in which I made choice to read the life of Luther. ... I did the more willingly read it, because he is generally branded with ambition, which caused him to do what he did, and that the Papists do so generally upbraid us that we cannot tell where our religion was before Luther; and some have taxed[2] him of an intemperate life. These reasons made me desire to read his life, to see upon what ground these opinions were built; and finding such satisfaction to myself, how falsely these were raised, I put it into English, and here enclosed have sent it you. It is not all his life, for I put no more into English than was not in the *Book of Martyrs*.[3]

These things of note I find in it. Firstly, what Luther acknowledges, he was instructed in the truth by an old man, who led him to the doctrine of justification by faith in Christ.[4]

---

[1] Brilliana Harley, Letter XL to Edward Harley in *Letters of the Lady Brilliana Harley*, 51–53.

[2] Here Brilliana used the verb "tax" with the meaning of "to accuse."

[3] A reference to John Foxe's (1516–1587) *Book of Martyrs*.

[4] Brilliana probably had in mind Johann von Staupitz (c.1460–1524), the Vicar-General of the Augustinian order of monks in Germany, of which Luther was a member. "If it had not been for Dr. Staupitz," Luther said on one occasion, "I should have sunk in hell" (cited Roland H. Bainton, *Here I*

And Erasmus, when his opinion was asked of Luther, said he was in the right. It is true the truth was much obscured with error; and then it pleased the Lord to raise up Luther as a trumpet to proclaim his truth and as a standard-bearer to hold out the ensign of his truth, which did but make those to appear of the Lord's side, who were so before. And it is apparent to me, that no ambitious ends moved Luther; for in all the course of his life he never showed ambition. Tho[ugh] he loved learning, yet, as far as I can observe, he never affected to be esteemed more learned than he was. So that in Luther we see our own faces. They that stand for the old true way they bring up new doctrine, and it is ambition, under the vail of religion.

Another observation I find in Luther, that all his fasting and strictness, in the way of popery, never gave him peace of conscience; for he had great fears till he had thoroughly learned the doctrine of justification by Christ alone. And so it will be with us all; no peace shall we have in our own righteousness.

And one thing more I must tell you, that I am not of their mind who think, if he had been of a milder temper it had been better; and so Erasmus says. But I think no other spirit could have served his turn. He was to cry aloud, like a trumpet; he was to have a Jonas spirit.[5]

Thus, my dear Ned, you may see how willingly I impart anything to you, in which I find any good. I may truly say, I never enjoy any thing that is good but presently my thoughts reflect upon you; but if anything that is evil befall me, I would willing bear it all myself, and so willingly would I bear

---

Stand: A Life of Martin Luther [New York, NY; Nashville, TN: Abingdon-Cokesbury Press, 1950], 53).

5 i.e., the spirit of Jonah. The Book of Jonah had been a favourite book of the Reformers.

the ill you should have, and rejoice that you should enjoy what is good. Your father is now at Hereford; I hope he will be at home tomorrow. Your brothers are well, and so are your sisters. ...

My dear Ned, I know you do not love medicines, yet I would fain have you drink, this May, some scurvy-grass[6] pounded and strained with beer, if there be any to be had in Oxford. It is a most excellent thing to purge the blood. ...

I have made a pie to send you; it is a kid[ney] pie. I believe you have not that meat ordinarily at Oxford; one half of the pie is seasoned with one kind of seasoning, and the other with another.

---

[6] Scurvy-grass has a flavour similar to watercress and its leaves are rich in Vitamin C.

William Whately (1583–1639)

Letter 25[1]

May 20, 1639

Dear Ned:

...When your father went to Hereford, he was not certain of his going to Banbury; and if he did, he meant to send on to let you know so much, that you might meet him on Saturday at Banbury, where I hope by God's mercy you will see your father; and I pray God you may both have a comfortable meeting; and tho[ugh] I cannot have part in it, yet absent, my desires are with you, and I hope in good time the Lord will give me the comfort of seeing you. ...

My dear Ned, I bless the Lord that in mercy he has so suited you with a tutor, upon whom your heart's desire is so much set. You might have had a good man, and not such a suitableness in him to your heart. I cannot blame you to fear the losing of him; for when we find any of like affections to us we ought to prize them, for they are not to be had every day.

As soon as I heard that Mr. Whately was sick,[2] my thoughts were that if Mr. Whately did die, Banbury men would desire to have Mr. Perkins. My poor prayers have been ever since I heard it, and shall be, that the Lord would guide your tutor in

---

[1] Brilliana Harley, Letter XLI to Edward Harley in *Letters of the Lady Brilliana Harley*, 54–55.

[2] William Whately (1583–1639) was a Puritan divine who had a lectureship in Banbury, where his preaching was enormously popular. Apparently, he was known to some as "the Roaring Boy of Banbury." Ned's fear was that if Whately died, which he did in 1639, his tutor, Edward Perkins, would be called in his place. On Whately, see Samuel Clark, *The Marrow of Ecclesiastical History*, 2nd ed. (London: T.U., 1654), 929–934.

the right way, most for his glory; and I hope the Lord will settle him in the place where he now is, for he must as well look how he leaves his standing as upon what ground he would accept of that place which is offered him. It is true his call to Banbury is right and just, but whether it be as right he should leave that standing in which he is, I know not.

I fear me that that has been the spoiling of the universities and corrupting of the gentry there bred, because that as soon as any man is come to any ripeness of judgement and holiness he is taken away, and so they still glean the garden of the ripe grapes and leave sour ones behind. My dear Ned, m[a]y God be blessed, who has given you a heart to look up to him, and a desire to depend on his most holy providence. And the Lord in mercy establish your heart in waiting on him, and then you will never be ashamed.

It is true that you no sooner peeped into the world but you had a taste of the various and changeableness of the conditions here below; for no sooner were you at Gloucester but you were removed, and from Shrewsbury.[3] But, as you well observe, for which I hope both you and I shall endeavour to be thankful, God still provided for you. And so I trust he will do still. My hope is, that you will still enjoy your worthy tutor, which will be much contentment to me. I hope your father will be a means to settle his thoughts.

I have here sent you a copy of a sermon preached in Scotland; you must take care who sees it; you never read such a piece. ... the Lord in mercy bless you, and fill you with his grace, and give you a feeling of his unspeakable love in Christ Jesus, that so you may be tied by the bonds of love to all obedience to your God.[4]

---

[3] A reference to his childhood education. Shrewsbury School had been founded by Edward VI in 1552. Ned had left Shrewsbury for Oxford in 1638.

[4] Cf. Brilliana Harley, Letter LXVI to Edward Harley, February 28, 1639/40, in *Letters of the Lady Brilliana Harley*, 83: "let the love of your God be the motive of all your obedience."

Letter 26[1]

July 5, 1639

Dear Ned:

... I bless God that you are well, and my dear Ned, be careful of yourself; be careful of the health of your body for my sake; and above all, be careful of the health of your soul for your own and my sake; and as to the body, those things do most hurt which are of a deadly quality as poison, so nothing hurts the soul like that deadly poison of sin.[2] Therefore, my dearest, be watchful against those great and subtle and vigilant enemies of your precious soul.

I believe you know that one of the best parts of a soldier is to stand upon his guard, and his greatest shame (next to running away) not to be found so. So is it in our spiritual warfare. If Satan surprise us, he takes us at his will, and if we turn our backs and run away, O! he will pursue till we be taken.[3]

---

[1] Brilliana Harley, Letter XLVI to Edward Harley in *Letters of the Lady Brilliana Harley*, 60–61.

[2] Cf. Brilliana Harley, Letter LIV to Edward Harley. November 4, 1639, in *Letters of the Lady Brilliana Harley*, 71: "O let it be your resolution and practice in your life, rather to die than sin against your gracious and holy God. We have so gracious a God, that nothing can put a distance between him and our souls, but sin; watch therefore against that enemy."

[3] Spiritual warfare was much on Brilliana's mind in the summer of 1639. As she wrote to Edward on June 21, 1639: "there is so much discourse of wars, that it may well put us in mind of our spiritual warfare. In both there is nothing more requisite than to stand upon the watch; to be surprised is both a shame and great disadvantage to a soldier. Therefore, dear Ned, stand as it were sentinel, and be sure you be not found sleeping; watch against your enemy, and the Lord of heaven, that neither comes so near sleep as to slumber, keep you in all safety" (Letter XLIII in *Letters of the Lady Brilliana Harley*, 57).

Thomas Goodwin (1600–1680)

Letter 27[1]

October 18, 1639

Dear Ned:

... the Lord bless you and give you that heavenly wisdom to remember your Creator in the days of your youth,[2] that you may serve your God with an upright heart, and the Lord in mercy teach you to profit in all the ways of wisdom, and lead you in the way in which you should walk. My dear Ned, omit not private duties, and stir up yourself to exercise yourself in holy conference; beg of God to give you a delight in speaking and thinking of those things which are your eternal treasure. I many times think godly conference is as much neglected by God's children, as any duty.[3] I am confident you will no ways neglect the opportunity of profiting in the ways of learning, and I pray God prosper your endeavours. ...

Remember my love to your worthy tutor, and still believe that I much rejoice when I can express myself to be

Your most affectionate mother, Brilliana Harley.

My cousin Davis presents her service to you.[4]

---

[1] Brilliana Harley, Letter XLIX to Edward Harley in *Letters of the Lady Brilliana Harley*, 64–66.

[2] A reference to Ecclesiastes 12:1.

[3] Brilliana is thinking about the importance of spiritual conversation with close friends as a key means of spiritual growth. See Letter 28.

[4] Brilliana's "cousin Davis" is probably related to Priamus Davies, on whom, see "An essay on the life and spirituality of Brilliana Harley."

I have sent you a basket of Stocking apples;[5] *there are 4 or 5 of another kind. I hope you will not despise them, coming from a friend, tho[ugh] they are not to be compared to Oxford apples.*

In the basket with the apples is The Return of Prayer.[6] *I could not find the place I spoke of to your tutor, when he was with me; but since, I found it, and have sent the book to you, that he may see it, and judge a little of it. For my part, I am not of that opinion, that God will not grant the prayer of others, for the want of our joining with the rest, or that God does stand upon such a number. But I am not peremptory, but upon good reason I hope I shall yield. But this I think and believe, that none join in prayer with others but those that sympathize one with another; for it is not the consenting to, but the earnest desiring of the same.*

---

5 Apples from the village of Stocking in Herefordshire.

6 This is almost definitely a reference to Thomas Goodwin's (1600–1680) treatise, *The Returne of Prayers* (London: R. Dawlman and L. Fawne, 1636). In chapter 4 of this treatise (72–85), Goodwin deals with the question of corporate prayer where he states, "If thy heart did sympathize, and accord in the same holy affections with those others in praying, then it is certain thy voice hath helpt to carry it" (73). See the discussion by Johanna Harris, "'But I thinke and beleeve': Lady Brilliana Harley's Puritanism in Epistolary Community" in *The Intellectual Culture of Puritan Women, 1558–1680*, ed. Johanna Harris and Elizabeth Scott-Baumann (London: Palgrave Macmillan, 2010), 117–188.

Letter 28[1]

November 1, 1639

Dear Ned:

It is my joy that you are well, and I bless my God that you have had your health, which I was assured of this day by your letter, which is welcome to me. That the apples came well to your hand I am well pleased, and I hope you have made use of them for your dessert in your chamber. ...

My fear is that we should fall into the same error as Calvin did, who was so earnest in opposing the popish holy days that he entrenched upon the holy Sabbath,[2] so I fear we shall be

---

[1] Brilliana Harley, Letter LIII to Edward Harley in *Letters of the Lady Brilliana Harley*, 68–70.

[2] Despite their indebtedness to John Calvin in numerous areas of Christian thought and piety, the Puritans did not follow him in their thinking about the Lord's Day. While Calvin supported the practice of meeting on the Lord's Day for worship, he did not equate Sunday with the Jewish Sabbath. For an extremely helpful study of the origins of Puritan Sabbatarianism, see John H. Primus, *Holy Time: Moderate Puritanism and the Sabbath* (Macon, GA: Mercer University Press, 1989). In the words of J.I. Packer, it was the Puritans who "created the English Christian Sunday (*A Quest for Godliness: The Puritan Vision of the Christian Life* [Wheaton, IL: Crossway Books, 1990], 235). In this context, it appears that Brilliana is responding to those who would dispense with the Book of Common Prayer altogether and the danger, in making such a response, of uncritically endorsing the Book of Common Prayer in all of its details. See Levy, "Perceptions and Beliefs," 171.

For a classic Puritan work on the Lord's Day as the Sabbath, see John Ley, *Sunday a Sabbath. Or, A Preparative Discourse for discussion of Sabbatary doubts* (London: George Lathum, 1641). It is interesting that Calvin is cited in defence of Ley's views ("The Preface to the Reader" in *Sunday a Sabbath*, C[4] recto). The year following the publication of this work, Ley dedicated a funeral sermon to Brilliana. See Appendix 3.

so earnest in beating down their too much vilifying of the Common Prayer Book, that we shall say more for it than ever we intended.

My dear Ned, keep always a watch over your precious soul; tie yourself to a daily self-examination; think over the company you have been in, and what your discourse was, and how you found yourself affected, how in the discourses of religion; observe what knowledge you were able to express, and with what affection to it, and where you find yourself to come short, labour to repair that want; if it be in knowledge of any point, read something that may inform you in what you find you know not; if the fault be in affection, that you find a weariness in that discourse of religion, go to God, beg of him new affections to love those things which by nature we cannot love. After discourse, call to mind whether you have been too apt to take exceptions, or whether any have provoked you, and examine yourself how you took it.

My dear Ned, ... this is the rule I take with myself, and I think it is the best way to be acquainted with our own heart, for we know not what is in us, till occasions and temptation draws out that matter which lays quiet; and in a due observation, we shall find at last, in what we are proud, in what fearful, and what will vex and eat our hearts with care and grief. I can speak it of myself. There are many things which I see wise men and women trouble themselves with, that I bless my gracious God for they never touched my heart; but I will not clear myself, for there are some things that of myself I can not bear them. So that if I should have only observed myself in some things, should think I were of so settled a mind I would not be moved; but I know there are blasts that trouble any calm, which is not settled upon that Rock, which is higher than ourselves.

Letter 28

My dear Ned, I will not excuse my length of lines, tho[ugh] it maybe you may think it too long a letter; but rather think upon the affection with which I write it, who am
Your most affectionate mother, Brilliana Harley.

… Remember my love to your worthy tutor.
Your father, I thank God, came well home to night late.

Letter 29[1]

January 31, 1639/40

Dear Ned:

It hath pleased God that I have been ill ever since you went; but yet I rejoice in God's mercy to me, that you enjoy your health, which your letters have assured me of. I thank you for them, for they have been sweet refreshments to me. Your letter this week by the carrier I received last night, and I bless God that I received such childlike expressions of love from you. I hope I receive the fruit of your prayers, for the Lord hath been pleased to shew his strength in my weakness to enable me to undergo such a fit of weakness, which hath made stronger bodies than mine to stoop.

This day seven at night it pleased God I did miscarry, which I did desire to have prevented; but the Lord which brought his own work to pass, and I desired to submit to it. Your father out of his tender care over me sent for Doctor Diodati,[2] who gave me some directions, and is now gone. I

---

[1] Brilliana Harley, Letter LX to Edward Harley in *Letters of the Lady Brilliana Harley*, 78–79.

[2] The London physician Theodore Diodati (1573–1651), who was able to maintain a practice that included a number of aristocratic families as far north as Lancashire. Brilliana spells his name as either Dayodet and Deodate, which indicates that he had Anglicised the pronunciation of his surname. On Diodati and his visits to Brilliana, see Donald Clayton Dorian, *The English Diodatis* (New Brunswick, NJ: Rutgers University Press, 1950), 184–193; Henry Connor, "Lady Brilliana Harley (1598–1643): Her medicines and her doctors," *Journal of Medical Biography* 24, no.1 (2016): 130–131, 133–134. His brother was the Genevan divine, Giovanni Diodati (1576–1649), who was

thank God I am pretty well, and I hope that as the Lord hath strengthened me to bear my weakness in my bed, so I trust he will enable me to rise out of my bed. I was so desirous that you should know how I was, that I entreated your father to let you know in what condition I was.

---

one of the authors of the Canons of Dordt. His son Charles (1609–1638) was a close friend of John Milton (1608–1674).

Letter 30[1]

June 20, 1642

My dear Ned:

... This day Mr. Yates[2] came from Hereford, where he went to preach, by the entreaty of some in the town, and this befell him. When he had ended his prayer before the sermon, which he was short in, because he was loth to tire them, 2 men went out of the church and cried "pray God bless the King; this man does not pray for the king." Upon which, before he read his text, he told them that ministers had that liberty, to pray before or after the sermon for the church and state; for all that, they went to the bells and rang [them], and a great many went into the church-yard and cried "Roundheads," and some said, "let us cast stones at him!" And he could not look out of doors ..., but they cried, "Roundhead."[3]

---

[1] Brilliana Harley, Letter CLXV to Edward Harley in *Letters of the Lady Brilliana Harley*, 170–171.

[2] Robert Harley had been instrumental in the appointment of John Yates as the rector of Leintwardine. The transcription of this letter by Thomas Taylor Lewis has the name "Mr. Davis." On the basis of manuscript evidence, Jacqueline Susan Levy has argued that this must be a transcription error and the near riot involved John Yates, the rector of Leintwardine. See Jacqueline Susan Levy, "Perceptions and Beliefs: The Harleys of Brampton Bryan and the Origins and Outbreak of the English Civil War" (PhD thesis, London University, 1983), 271–272 and n.91. See also Eales, *Puritans and Roundheads*, 145, n.56. For the letter with Yates' name in it, see *Manuscripts of His Grace the Duke of Portland*, III, 103.

[3] The term "Roundhead" had its origins in the final days of 1641 as a derisive term for adherents of the Parliamentary party. For details of its origin, see "Roundhead," *The Encyclopædia Britannica*, 11th ed. (New York, NY: Encyclopædia Britannica, Inc., 1911), 23:772; Eales, *Puritans and Roundheads*,

In the afternoon they would not let him preach; so he went to the cathedral. Those that had any goodness were much troubled and weep much.

---

143. Cf. also Brilliana Harley, Letter CLXI to Edward Harley, June 4, 1642, in *Letters of the Lady Brilliana Harley*, 167, where Brilliana mentioned the setting-up of a maypole in nearby Ludlow and "a thing like a head upon it." According to Brilliana, a great number of people gathered around it as a number of them "shot at it in derision of Roundheads." Also see Brilliana Harley, Letter CLXVI to Edward Harley, June 24, 1642, in *Letters of the Lady Brilliana Harley*, 172.

Letter 31[1]

July 19, 1642

My dear Ned:

I long to see you, but would not have you come down, for I cannot think this country very safe. By the papers I have sent to your father, you will know the temper of it. I hope your father will give me full directions how I may best have my house guarded, if need be; if he will give the directions, I hope, I shall follow it.

My dear Ned, I thank God I am not afraid. It is the Lord's cause that we have stood for, and I trust, though our iniquities testify against us, yet the Lord will work for his own name sake, and that he will now show the men of the world that it is hard fighting against heaven. And for our comforts,[2] I think never any laid plots to rout out all God's children at once, but that the Lord did show himself mighty in saving his servants and confounding his enemies, as he did Pharaoh, when he thought to have destroyed all Israeli, and so Haman. Now, the intention is, to rout out all that fear God, and surely the Lord will arise to help us: and in your God let your confidence be, and I am assured it is so.

---

[1] Brilliana Harley, Letter CLXXVII to Edward Harley in *Letters of the Lady Brilliana Harley*, 180–181.

[2] Brilliana is using the word "comfort" in the now-obsolete meaning of "strengthening," "succour" or "support."

Puritan spirituality in the letters of Brilliana Harley

One met Samuel[3] and not knowing where he dwelt, Samuel told him he was a Derbyshire man, and that he came lately from thence ...; the papist told him, that there was but a few Puritans in this country, and 40 men would cut them all off.

Had I not had this occasion to send to your father, yet I had sent this boy[4] up to London; he is such a roguish boy that I dare not keep him in my house, and as little do I dare to let him go in this country, least he join with the company of volunteers, or some other such crew. I have given him no more money than will serve to bear his charges up. And because I would have him make haste and be sure to go to London, I have told him, that you will give him something for his pains, if he come to you in good time and do not loiter. And here enclosed I have sent you half a crown. Give him what you think fit, and I desire he may not come down anymore, but that he may be persuaded to go to sea, or some other employment. He thinks he shall come down again. Good Ned, do not tell Martin that I send him up with such an intention.

I have directed these letters to you, and I send him to you, because I would not have the country take notice, that I send to your father so often; but when such occasions come, I must

---

3 Samuel was one of the household servants in the employment of the Harleys. He often conveyed Brilliana's letters to her son and those of Edward to his mother: see Letter CLV to Edward Harley, May 19, 1642, in *Letters of the Lady Brilliana Harley*, 162; Letter CLIX to Edward Harley, May 28, 1642, in *Letters of the Lady Brilliana Harley*, 166.

One piece of advice with regard to the employment of servants that Brilliana gave to her son was to be cautious about hiring young men and boys (Letter CXIX, May 22, 1641, in *Letters of the Lady Brilliana Harley*, 132). Samuel would appear to have fallen into this category. Brilliana noted in this letter that he had a "sour nature," something that irked her. A couple of years earlier, she had told Ned, "I think to live with a sour nature is a greater pain then to be fed always with sour and bitter meat, and to have the smoke in one's eyes; for my part, I love no sourness, and I hope you are of my mind in that; yet it has been my lot to meet with some of that disposition." (Letter XLVIII, July 20, 1639, in *Letters of the Lady Brilliana Harley*, 63).

4 Another young servant by the name of Martin.

needs send to him, for I can rely upon nobody's counsel but his. I pray God bless you and preserve you in safety ...

My cousin Davis[5] tells me that none can make shot but those whose trade it is, so I have made the plumber write to Worcester for 50 weight of shot. I sent to Worcester because I would not have it known. If your father think that is not enough, I shall send for more.

---

5 Probably Priamus Davies.

Letter 32[1]

July 2, 1642

My dear Ned:
I must needs thank you for your two letters this week; for, believe me, in this troublesome time and your father's absence and yours, your letters are of much comfort to me.

My dear Ned, at first when I saw how outrageously this country carried themselves against your father, my anger was so up, and my sorrow, that I had hardly patience to stay. But now, I have well considered, if I go away I shall leave all that your father has to the prey of our enemies, which they would be glad of; so that, and please God, I purpose to stay as long as it is possible, if I live. And this is my resolution, without your father contradict it.

I cannot make a better use of my life, next to serving my God, than do what good I can for you. ... It is very late, therefore I can say no more; but I pray God bless you with all his blessings, and I hope you will always be the joy of your

Most affectionate mother, Brilliana Harley.

---

[1] Brilliana Harley, Letter CLXXIX to Edward Harley, in *Letters of the Lady Brilliana Harley*, 182–183.

Letters 33-34[1]

August 18, 1642

Most worthy friend:
I had rather entreat a kindness from you than from any I know, assuring myself you will do the same to me, in whom you have as much interest in, as in any.

---

[1] Brilliana Harley, Letters CLXXX–CLXXXI to Edward Harley, in *Letters of the Lady Brilliana Harley*, 183–185. These two letters were to Ann Walcot (1603–1675), the wife of Humphrey Walcot (1586–1650) of Walcot, Shropshire. Any hopes that Brilliana had of repaying the debt soon after she had received the money were quickly dashed. Her Royalist neighbours blocked the payment of any of the rents from the Harley properties (Brilliana Harley, Letters CLXXIV and CLXXXV to Edward Harley, January 28, 1643 and February 14, 1643, in *Letters of the Lady Brilliana Harley*, 187–188). Thus, owing to Brilliana's death, the exigencies of the Civil Wars, and the financial challenges that Robert Harley faced during the Civil Wars and the Interregnum—in 1646, he estimated that his financial losses amounted to £12,990 (*Letters of the Lady Brilliana Harley*, 230)—it was not until 1682 that Edward Harley finally repaid the loan to the Walcot family. For details, see *Letters of the Lady Brilliana Harley*, 184–185, note *.

On Humphrey and Ann Walcot, see John R. Burton, "The Sequestration Papers of Humphrey Walcot," *Transactions of the Shropshire Archæological and Natural History Society* 3rd Series, 5 (1905): 313–328. See also Thomas Froysell, *The Gale of Opportunity. Or, A Sermon Preached (at Lidbury-North) at the Funerall of the Worshipfull Humphrey Walcot* (London: Thomas Parkhurst, 1658), 110–118. Froysell had preached this sermon in 1650 at the time of Humphrey Walcot's funeral. As noted in "An essay on the life and spirituality of Brilliana Harley," Froysell also preached Robert Harley's funeral sermon in 1656.

This published sermon for Walcot was a classic expression of Puritan piety. For instance, Froysell maintained: "*Qui non zelat, non amat.* He that hath not zeal for Christ, hath not love to Christ. True zeal is a seal of our election. Strictness and exactness is the beauty and lustre of religion. I say, you cannot do too much for Jesus Christ, he hath done so much for us" ("To his Highly Honored Mr John Walcot of Walcot Esquire" in *Gale of Opportunity*, B1 recto).

I have had of late in the mending of the leads of my house been enforced to lay out an extraordinary sum of money; and Edward Dally[2] with others, owing me rent, I cannot as yet get it. If you can lend me £40 for half or a quarter of a year, I shall take it as a great kindness, and I will pay the interest of it with all my heart, and give you any security my son and I can give you, which I hope will be enough for a greater sum. So, recommending you unto the protection of God, I rest,

Your most affectionate friend, Brilliana Harley.

August 22, 1642

My much honoured and dear friend:
I acknowledge this as a great favour, and I shall be ready to express my thanks with all the testimony of true respects, and I acknowledge, that for the virtues you have, I much love and honour you. I have received the £20 you are pleased to lend me, and I have made a bill of the receipt of it, and my son and myself have put our hands to the receipt of it, and I will, and please God, pay you very shortly. I desire to have my service presented to Mr. Walcot and your son; and desire you to believe that I am most unfeignedly

Your most affectionate friend, Brilliana Harley.

---

2 Edward Dally was one of the Harleys' tenants in Kingsland. In 1640, rent from this property gave the Harleys £460 per annum. See Eales, *Puritans and Roundheads*, 32.

Letter 35[1]

March 8, 1642/43

[To Robert Harley]

I send you this letter that you may know how I am and that I may know of you what I had best do. I enclose a copy of the paper Mr. Coningsby sent and a copy of my answer.[2] I hear my answer was sent on the Sabbath to Lord Herbert,[3] who I hear, has appointed six hundred soldiers and two pieces of ordnance to come against me, which some say will be at Brampton to-morrow, and some next week. We are all very cheerful and not afraid.

Let me know whether you think it best for me to stay at Brampton or whether I had best steal as many of the beasts and horses as I can and so go to some other place. I pray you do not make any fear of mine any ground of your resolution, but I desire to do that which is best in the opinion of those who can best judge. ...

---

[1] In *Manuscripts of His Grace the Duke of Portland*, III, 106.

[2] Fitzwilliam Coningsby (1589–1666) was the Royalist Governor of Hereford and had received orders from Charles I in January of 1642/43 to launch an assault on Brampton Byran. See Eales, *Puritans and Roundheads*, 165. For the March 1642/43 correspondence between Coningsby and Brilliana in this regard, see *Manuscripts of His Grace the Duke of Portland*, III, 105.

On January 17, 1642/43, Brilliana had told her husband that neither Coningsby nor John Scudamore "shows me any common kindness. I believe they thirst after my life and my children's. I do not see how I can stay with safety, for they threaten to put soldiers into my house. I believe you do not imagine how they use me" (*Manuscripts of His Grace the Duke of Portland*, III, 103).

[3] Edward Somerset (1602/3–1667), Lord Herbert of Raglan.

They have taken ten horses from me. I am sure they may as well do the greatest violence to the most innocent person as do what they do to me for I offend nobody.

Letter 36[1]

July 26, 1643

To Henry Lingen, High Sheriff, Sir Walter Pye, and Mr. Smallman

Your relations to me which you are pleased to make mention of might have invited you to another piece of service than this that you are now come upon, in which if you should have your desire it would never crown you with honour before men, nor blessings from God. For Sir William Vavasour's drawing his forces before my house by the King's command, I dare not, I cannot, I must not, believe it, since it has pleased our most gracious King to make many solemn promises that he would maintain the laws and liberties of this kingdom. I cannot then think he would give a command to take away anything from his loyal subjects, and much less to take away my house. If Sir William Vavasour will do so I must endeavour to keep what is mine as well as I can, in which I have the law of nature, of reason, and of the land on my side, and you none to take it from me. For Bristol and Gloucester, it is no precedent to me if they are taken, that I

---

[1] In *Calendar of the Manuscripts*, I, 8. Henry Lingen (1612–1662) was the High Sherriff of Herefordshire in 1643 and distantly related to the Harleys. Sir Walter Pye (1610–1659) was an MP for Herefordshire during the Short Parliament of 1640 and High Steward of Leominster. William Smallman (c.1615–1643) was MP for Leominster during the Short Parliament. For William Vavasour, see "An essay on the life and spirituality of Brilliana Harley."

should give away what is mine. I believe I shall have more comfort in keeping my own to the utmost, than ever you will have in the least endeavour to take it away.

Letter 37[1]

July 31, 1643

To Sir William Vavasour:
For my servants laying down their arms I know of none they bear but for mine and their defence, a thing warranted by the laws of the land, and it is strange to me that my having a few arms in my house is more offensive than [in] Sir John Winter's house.[2] Sir, for me to yield that you should place a garrison in my house, I cannot find out any reason for it, and under what notion you would do it, I know not; but this I conceive, I should become a prisoner in my own house, which I cannot yield to, for so I should speak myself guilty; and thus much more I must say, my dear husband hath entrusted me with his house and children, and therefore I cannot dispose of his house but according to his pleasure, and I do not know it is his pleasure that I should entertain soldiers in his house; and surely Sir, I never will voluntarily betray the trust my husband reposeth in me.

I have hitherto believed very well of you, and that I may do so, I will not—if I can help it—try how your soldiers will deal with me; and I trust the Lord my God will deliver me and mine out of all my enemies' hands; but if it hath pleased the Lord to appoint that your cruelties and wrongs to me and mine, and some of the inhabitants of this town, must

---

[1] In *Calendar of the Manuscripts*, I, 12–13.
[2] John Winter (*c.*1600–*c.*1673) was an ardent Roman Catholic, Royalist and secretary to the Queen, Henrietta Maria.

help to fill up the measure of all the cruelties now used against those that desire to keep faith in a good conscience, I shall not be displeased; for when the measure of cruelties is full, the day of deliverance will soon appear to the Church of God which is now afflicted.

And Sir, let me desire of you not to be displeased if I put you in mind with the rest of the gentlemen of this county, how you make yourselves guilty of innocent blood; for so you will, if you shed the least drop of any one with me.

Letter 38[1]

[August 1643]

The humble petition of Dame Brilliana Harley [to King Charles I]

Humbly showeth that your poor and distressed subject perceiveth by a gracious letter dated 21st of August from your sacred Majesty directed to your said subject and brought by Sir John Scudamore, knight, that many unjust informations have been given to your Majesty against your said subject. Be pleased therefore, gracious sovereign, to believe me, that my house is not nor never was, to my knowledge, a receptacle for any disloyal person, nor was my condition such, as to be a terror to any, much less did any by my command or privity either kill any of your Majesty's subjects, or fire any houses, or commit any outrages to bring or cause the forces under the command of Sir William Vavasour against me, but only kept such a number of servants with arms as in these woeful times might defend me against pillaging and plundering, a thing your Majesty hath in several proclamations expressed your dislike of.

Yet so it is, most gracious sovereign, that I have had servants imprisoned, some killed, and now by Sir William Vavasour's forces, all my horses, cattle, corn and other things taken away; my house attempted with many soldiers, horse and foot, with five or six cannons battering the walls, and almost every day assaulted by small shot, whereas your poor subject

---

[1] In *Calendar of the Manuscripts*, I, 17.

Brampton Bryan Castle today

did never offend your Majesty, or ever take up arms against your Majesty, or any man of mine, or any by mine appointment was in actual rebellion against your sacred Majesty. And therefore your poor subject hopeth and prayeth the premises being graciously weighed, your Majesty will not require that from me which by the law of the land is mine, and which if I shall give up, I have no subsistence for myself and mine. But that your Majesty will be pleased to command Sir William Vavasour to withdraw his forces and restore to me my goods, but if your Majesty will—notwithstanding the premises—command me out of my house, my humble desire is that you will in your clemency allow unto me some maintenances for me and mine and fit time to remove myself and family by your protection to pass to some other place where we may find subsistence, that we perish not. So shall she, who ever hath been and ever will be your loyal and faithful subject, pray for your sacred Majesty.

Appendices

Thomas Gataker, *Opera Gatakeri* (1680), frontispiece

Appendix 1

Thomas Gataker, "To the Right Worshipful, and his loving Kinsman, Sir Robert Harley, Knight of the Bath; And to the right worthy and religious, the Lady Brilliana his wife"[1]

1623

Right Worshipful: A former sermon of mine concerning matter of marriage being now the second time called for to pass the press, instead of adding to that, which some desired, I was advised and requested rather by others to annex this. Whereunto having yielded, I knew not which way better to direct it than to yourselves; at whose happy conjunction some part of it was preached, the residue through straits of time being for that time suppressed. What then you should have heard, if the time had permitted, both yourselves may now read (if you please) with some further enlargement, and others also (if they think it may be of use to them) under your names. Therein, as in a glass, as you, worthy Madam, may (I doubt not) see yourself lively deciphered; so you, blessed sir, yea

---

[1] In Thomas Gataker, *A Good Wife Gods Gift: and, A Wife Indeed. Two Mariage Sermons* (London: Fulke Clifton, 1623), (E) recto–[E2] verso. This was an unusual book for the publisher, Fulke Clifton (fl.1620–1644), to publish, since he specialized in broadsides and political pamphlets.

thrice blessed in this your happy choice,[2] might learn, but that (I know) you are not now to learn it, what a precious jewel God hath in her bestowed on you, and how great a measure of thankfulness you owe to him for his mercy to you therein.

Yea both of you may behold here, what a blessed estate and condition of life it is, that God hath pleased to call you unto, where the same is managed through his grace according to his will; notwithstanding those vile and foul aspersions here in part laid open, that those of that Romish faction are wont to cast upon it. If of those that abuse this holy and divine Ordinance, and carry themselves otherwise therein than they ought, there seem to any a Censure over-harsh here to be passed. Let them consider that it is no other than God's Word giveth good warrant for; and let them take heed, lest by censuring it, they give suspicion that themselves come within compass of such censure.

To yourselves (I am assured) no apology shall need either for it, or mine addressing it to you. But hoping it will be accepted, as it is intended, as a testimony of my sincere and entire affection to you both. With hearty prayers to God for your happy cohabitation to be long continued to his greater glory, your mutual comfort, and the further benefit of those that may have dependence upon you, I commend you to him, and his gracious Word,[3] who vouchsafes thereby to build you further in those good graces that he hath begun in you, that you may have inheritance with those that are here truly sanctified, and shall hereafter be eternally saved. Amen.

Your Worships to be commended in the Lord, Tho[mas] Gataker.

---

[2] A reference to the fact that Robert's marriage to Brilliana was his third.
[3] Cf. Acts 20:32. This verse was placed in the margin at this point in the text.

Appendix 2

Robert Horn, "To the Noble Lady, the Lady Harley, the pious consort of that religious knight, Sir Robert Harley of Brampton in Herefordshire"[1]

1632

Christian Lady:

I present you (here) with some fruits of my age, the root (out of which they sprung) standeth in that famous history of a woman of rare faith; and because a woman, therefore the fitter to be commended to you, and this for the truth's sake that dwelleth in you. This truth is that noble guest that takes up lodging nowhere, but in a heart, such as is according to the faith of God's elect. Such a room of special receipt it hath found in you long: a chamber or room trimmed for a daughter of heaven, so highly born. And for this, you are the observation and speech of many, and the grace of God in you, which (though now offered to the eye) is not so much to show what you are in a right understanding, as to set you further forward to the prize of that high calling, at which you aim, and not at things by the way, the aim of those that

---

[1] Robert Horn, "The Epistle Dedicatory" in *The History of the Woman of Great Faith* (London: Philemon Stephens and Chr. Meridith, 1632).

delight to be blown up with the winds of praise, for what they do well. Worthy Madam, you have run well, few of your sex and sort better. Keep on as you do, there is no standing till you be as your Father in heaven would have you to be, perfect as he is (Matthew 5:48).

Here are the steps of faith in a woman, a Canaanite: tread in them, and you are sure of your way. In this you go not alone, and you have a worthy leader. Your dearest husband is he, who (being the guide of your life, and to your precious faith a most able coadjutor) doth by his godly precedence, chalk you the way for your safer going on. And if I shall, by the blessing of God upon that which is here done, be vouchsafed worthy to add, though the least grain of improvement to the aright ordering of your steps in this way of faith, I shall think my labour and desires very happy, and the same highly advanced. And now for this, and for the sweet children of your body, likewise for the parent of them, your most loving husband, and my most kind patron, I do, and still pray, who am, your good Ladyship, very greatly bounden for the service of your faith, Robert Horn.

Appendix 3

John Ley,
"To the Honourable the Lady Brilliana Harley and to the Right Worshipfull the Lady Alice Lucie, two truly virtuous and Religious Ladies"[1]

1640

Right worthy and much honoured Ladies, I doubt not but (as elect Ladies) your names are registered in the Book of Life, and I cannot but conceive (were you acquainted with each other as I am with you both) you would much desire to be as near in place for Christian communion as you are in name in this dedication, wherein you have a double right, the one from the argument (a gracious matron like yourselves, though in secular respects of a lower sphere), the other from the author, who oweth a public attestation to your manifold virtues for inducement to others to value divine grace above human greatness, as your Ladyships do. To which purpose

---

[1] John Ley, "To the Honourable the Lady Brilliana Harley and to the Right Worshipfull the Lady Alice Lucie, two truly virtuous and Religious Ladies" in his *A patterne of Pietie. Or The Religious life and death of that Grave and gracious matron, Mrs. Jane Ratcliffe Widow and Citizen of Chester* (London: Richard Bostocke, 1640), A3 recto–[A5] recto. John Ley (1583–1662), a lecturer at St. Peter's Church in Chester, served as a member of the Westminster Assembly and was regarded in his day as a pillar of Presbyterianism.

the example I now exhibit may (and I trust will) do some acceptable service.

It is (I doubt not) one part of the happy communion of saints here on earth, that the living may (and many times do) reap good from the godly by reading of their goodness when they are dead, though while they lived they never knew them. I have therefore presented to common view the representation of an excellent pattern of Christian piety of your own sex, who is the sacred and sad subject of the discourse ensuing: sacred in regard of the excellent graces wherewith this daughter of our heavenly Father was endowed, and sad to those who derived daily fruit from her example and society, and now by her death are deprived of them both.

And I do it under your worthy names both that (besides the invitation of others to imitation of your virtues) I may profess mine own gratitude, whereto your favours have much engaged me, and may point the readers in your persons to such a proof of piety as (with all that know you) may lead them to a belief of what I report of her they knew not, at least as probable and like to be true. But for those who had opportunity for immediate observation of what she was, and how she lived, I cannot from them look for any less than assured assent to what my tongue in part before, and now mine hand, fully hath testified of her.

If the divine providence had so disposed of your dwellings that you might have consorted with her oft enough to be sufficiently acquainted, your Charity, I persuade myself, would have readily descended to the society of dear sisters of such a saint, as her humility would have done to the office of a servant of such excellent ladies, and you would have mutually communicated together with no less truth and strength of affection in your kind (notwithstanding the note of infirmity made upon it) than David and Jonathan did in theirs.

Appendix 3

It is a rare thing in your rank[2] to be so really religious, whereby your second birth shineth the more by reflex from your first, and as rare, for such as are so religious to be both in judgement and affection so free from prejudice and partial acceptation of any, as to esteem of all rather according to their sincerity in weighty duties, than to accept to their scrupulousness in matter of smallest importance.

There are some whose zeal ... is so vehemently set upon worthless trifles, as if they were matters of greatest moment; and others whose antipathy is as adverse to some harmless things which have no fault at all but in the fancy of those that mistake them; from both which extremes your Ladyships have (as she did while she lived) kept a reasonable distance. And so your respects both to preachers and people have been uniformly carried with religious favour, without any complement to irregular faction.

This is to make such an happy union of piety and peace here below, as will at last unite you in God in everlasting fruition of the felicity above; and in that way (the King of Kings' highway to heaven) my heartiest prayers and praises to God shall attend on your piety and prudence, and my best service be dedicated to the acceptance of you both, who by the just dessert of your own great worth, and my due debt for undeserved demonstrations of respect, have obliged me to remain

Your Ladyships' most sincerely devoted servant,
John Ley.

---

[2] 1 Corinthians 1:26 is cited in the margin at this point.

Charles I (1600–1649)

Appendix 4

Charles I's letter to Lady Brilliana Harley[1]

August 21, 1643
The Court at Matson

Whereas we understand that Brampton Bryan Castle in our county of Hereford hath been and is made a receptacle and place of retreat to the rebels now in arms against us, and a great terror to the country thereabouts by killing of divers of our good subjects, firing of houses and many other outrages, and hath been in a rebellious manner maintained and defended against our forces; yet being very desirous to believe that what hath been done in and from your said Castle hath rather proceeded from your being seduced by evil counsel than out of your ill-affection to us and our service, and being willing to avoid effusion of blood, and unwilling that our forces—in respect of your sex and condition—should take such course for forcing or firing of the same as they must otherwise be compelled to take; for these reasons we have sent our trusty and well-beloved Sir John Scudamore,[2] knight, in our name to demand the said castle to be immediately surrendered to us, and we do hereby advise and require you to admit of our forces into the same under the

---

[1] In *Calendar of the Manuscripts*, I, 14.
[2] On Scudamore, see Letter 12.

An illustration of the ruins of Brampton Bryan in John Webb and T.W. Webb, *Memorials of the Civil War Between King Charles I and the Parliament of England as it Affected Herefordshire and the Adjacent Counties* (London: Longmans, Green, and Co., 1879), II, 14

conduct of Sir William Vavasour, knight, or such as he shall appoint, for the safety and security of that country, assuring you in the word of a King of our grace and free pardon for the offences aforesaid in case the said Castle be immediately delivered according to these our commands; but if you shall refuse to obey this our command and advice in so particular and gracious a manner directed to you, you must thank yourself for that ruin and destruction which contrary to our desire will unavoidably involve you; and so expecting your ready compliance, as well in order to your interest, as to your loyalty, we bid you heartily farewell.

Discover other titles from Heritage Seminary Press

Paul and His Christian Mission
By Michael Azad A.G. Haykin
Includes Study Guide

The mission of the apostle Paul is central to the New Testament, where it was vital in the establishment of the early church and spreading the gospel throughout the world of his day. This study provides a concise but rich view of Paul the man and Paul the missionary. At his conversion to Christ, Paul was given a clear mandate to bring the gospel to the Gentiles. Paul loved the church, and he was zealous to win the lost to Christ. He appreciated and cultivated co-labourers in the work of the gospel, as he depended on the power of the Holy Spirit.

Paul's experience challenges the reader. Study guide questions are provided to help reflect on and apply the things that are learned in this short, focused study of Paul's life.

ISBN 978-1-77484-106-8 (Pbk)
ISBN 978-1-77484-107-5 (Ebook)
88 pages; 5.5 x 8.5"
Published December 2022

An imprint of H&E Publishing
hesedandemet.com

Discover other titles from Heritage Seminary Press

This Poor Man Called: Stories and Songs of David
Volume 1 & Volume 2
By David G. Barker

David Barker takes a unique approach in this exploration of the psalms of David. Each chapter begins with a creative retelling of the biblical narrative, setting the scene for the psalm arising out of that experience. Having grounded the psalm in the "story," Barker then goes into a verse-by-verse exposition of the psalm, and provides some explanatory notes and a statement of the key message of the psalm.

At the end of each psalm exposition, Barker asks three basic questions: What do we learn about God? What do we learn about ourselves as the people of God? and What do we learn about the world? Answering these questions helps us to understand how David's experience shaped his theocentric and biblical worldview.

Volume 1
ISBN 978-1-77484-063-4 (Pbk)
ISBN 978-1-77484-064-1 (Ebook)
122 pages; 5.5 x 8.5"
Published Spring 2022

Volume 2
ISBN 978-1-77484-110-5 (Pbk)
ISBN 978-1-77484-111-2 (Ebook)
192 pages; 5.5 x 8.5"
Published February 2023

An imprint of H&E Publishing
hesedandemet.com

Discover other titles from Heritage Seminary Press

Losing Your Luggage: Finding Freedom from Sinful Baggage
By Rick Reed

Losing Your Luggage takes you on a journey through Romans 6–8, helping you find freedom from the sinful baggage that weighs you down. Your guide for this trip is Rick Reed, who brings out practical, down-to-earth wisdom from Paul's letter as he walks alongside you on this journey. He is one who speaks from experience and is a helpful guide to show you the main sights and lessons of these important chapters. Journey toward greater joy and freedom in Christ—and lose some sinful baggage along the route!

ISBN 978-1-77484-120-4 (Pbk)
ISBN 978-1-77484-121-1 (Ebook)
104 pages; 6 x 9"
Published June 2023

An imprint of H&E Publishing
hesedandemet.com

Discover other titles from Heritage Seminary Press

Life is Worship: A *festschrift* in honour of Douglas A. Thomson
Editors: David G. Barker & Michael A.G. Haykin

These essays honour the life and ministry of Dr. Doug Thomson who, as a teacher, pastor, colleague and music leader, has influenced countless lives and congregations in Ontario, Canada, and beyond. The themes of these chapters cover themes that are precious in the life of the church—revealing how all of life is worship.

Topics include expositions of psalms and hymns, the theology of worship, spirituals, hallmarks of a worship leader, friendship in the composition of hymns, lament, etc.—even some sermons for Easter weekend. It is hoped that these essays will encourage discussion, promote the development of an understanding of the theology around worship, challenge readers to think deeply about this crucial area and, most of all, bring glory and praise to our great God.

ISBN 978-1-77484-128-0 (Pbk)
ISBN 978-1-77484-129-7 (Ebook)
364 pages; 6 x 9"
Published September 2023

HERITAGE SEMINARY PRESS

An imprint of H&E Publishing
hesedandemet.com

Dominus Deus fortitudo mea | The sovereign LORD is my strength

www.ingramcontent.com/pod-product-compliance
Lightning Source LLC
Chambersburg PA
CBHW060608080526
44585CB00013B/732